'This is a much-needed and timely book as society moves through these uncertain times our young people.

Presented as a series of nurturing and safe activities which build a sense of safety and s to explore aspects of anxiety, it will be an essential tool for any adult supporting young people to feel more confident, develop a positive self-image and overcome social anxiety.

The simple activities presented offer a "small steps" approach to beginning to understand where anxieties may be rooted and how these can be safely contained and managed through a positive focus on breathing, rhythm, sound and physical movement.

A must for all of those working with children and young people.'

Alison Chown, *Play Therapist, Supervisor, Specialist Practitioner in Social, Emotional, and Mental Health, and author*

'In this brilliant book, Sue Jennings brings a lifetime of experience working through the creative arts and dramatherapy to the support of children and young people experiencing social anxiety; it is a much-needed practical volume for them and their therapists. She introduces guided techniques to help the physical rhythms of the body with breathing and self-regulation, moving into dynamic approaches to the exploration of feelings and places of safety, where she shows how, when young people have control over their own imaginations, they can consciously bring themselves to a safer place of healing. Working with sequenced nurture-oriented Mandala exercises and stories, the young people's view of themselves is no longer dependent on others' opinions of them and can lead to a changed self-perception, employing masks and little theatres to consolidate further growth – all accompanied by worksheets, home handouts, and story texts mentioned throughout the book.'

Joanna Jaaniste, *Adjunct Fellow, Western Sydney University; Director of the Dramatherapy Centre, Sydney; PhD (Dementia and Dramatherapy), AThR (Drama)*

'Dr Sue Jennings has yet again produced a jewel in the crown of her eternally renowned Neuro-Dramatic-Play approach, incorporating Embodiment Projection Role and Theatre of Resilience, and it is a timely resource in these post-COVID times of rising anxiety. In this latest treasure trove, Sue's nurturing, caring way of being is evident as she guides us through a wealth of gentle activities that the facilitator can use with young people experiencing social anxiety and self-esteem issues. Her suggestion to allow the young people to choose the activities themselves along with the non-competitive, failsafe nature of the exercises ensure that they gain a sense of safety, control, independence, capability, belonging, and motivation – all important pillars of self-esteem. Sue's unwavering passion for supporting young people, along with her openness to embracing all modalities of therapy, ensures that this book will provide many gems of knowledge, support, and opportunities for facilitators and participants alike. I can't wait to use it.'

Ber Carroll, *Parent Mentor, Play Therapist and Sensory Attachment Intervention Practitioner; Tutor for University College Cork and for Children's Therapy Centre Ireland; Advanced Diploma in Neuro-Dramatic-Play*

'Who says social anxiety can only be dealt with seriously? Why don't we learn how to care for both ourselves and others via creative and artistic play as a way of response? In this fragmented era saturated with crisis and chaos, this precious and elegant guidebook by Dr Sue Jennings, full of both wisdom and fun, effectively introduces you to a playfully nurturing model that takes care of social anxiety by helping people to regulate and liberate themselves in a bottom-up and step-by-step manner, starting from settling in body through understanding feelings to re-activating vitality and spirit within and beyond oneself.

You can learn here about theories through practical techniques and practical techniques through theories.

It is also not just a piece of therapeutic work that tackles social anxiety as a problem, but a book of inspiration, rich in insights about human connection and trust in relation to play and artistic activities from which games, metaphors and rituals for growth, healing, and transformation arise.'

Ng Shiu Hei Larry (Larry Ng), *Dramatherapist, Certified Feldenkrais Method Teacher and Theatre Practitioner, Hong Kong*

'Dealing with anxiety could be a life challenge if not addressed properly and at early stages. Sue's book is a wonderful resource, whether you are supporting or teaching someone to manage anxiety or you are dealing with it yourself! Inside you will find a comprehensible and well-guided programme that goes from breathing and relaxation and builds up to theatre and storytelling. Filled with creativity and playfulness, it addresses anxiety in a way the brain understands best: welcoming, compassionate and nurturing.'

Ulises Moreno-Serena, *Coordinator at Teatro Aplicado CDMX, Mexico; MA (Psychology)*

Managing Social Anxiety in Children and Young People

Managing Social Anxiety in Children and Young People introduces a new approach for working with anxious children and young people to help them develop social skills and reduce stress.

Structured around the principles of 'nurturing and nesting', the book focuses on a practical approach which strays away from dependency on medicine, and relies on the stimulation of thoughts and feelings during the process of change. It shows readers how shifting perceptions of oneself and others can change a person's attitude. The chapters feature tangible resources and exercises for developing the core processes of breathing, rhythm, sound, and physical movement in a way that can lead to a reduction of anxiety and a new awareness of the self. The techniques are clearly laid out in developmental sequences, accompanied by illustrated worksheets and story sheets.

This book will be of interest to teachers, teaching assistants, care workers, clinicians, therapists, parents, and all professionals involved in the support and development of children and young people.

Sue Jennings is a Professor of Play (European Federation of Dramatherapists), the creator of Neuro-Dramatic-Play, and the author of 53 books. She has pioneered Dramatherapy and Play Therapy internationally. She is Senior Research Fellow at the Shakespeare Institute, University of Birmingham, UK, a Distinguished Scholar at the University of the Witwatersrand, South Africa, and an Honorary Fellow of the University of Roehampton, London.

Managing Social Anxiety in Children and Young People

Practical Activities for Reducing Stress and Building Self-esteem

Sue Jennings

Routledge
Taylor & Francis Group

LONDON AND NEW YORK

Cover image: created by Charlie Meyer

First published 2023
by Routledge
4 Park Square, Milton Park, Abingdon, Oxon OX14 4RN

and by Routledge
605 Third Avenue, New York, NY 10158

Routledge is an imprint of the Taylor & Francis Group, an informa business

British Library Cataloguing-in-Publication Data
A catalogue record for this book is available from the British Library

Library of Congress Cataloging-in-Publication Data
A catalog record has been requested for this book

ISBN: 9781032256665 (hbk)
ISBN: 9781032256634 (pbk)
ISBN: 9781032256641 (ebk)

DOI: 10.4324/9781032256641

Typeset in Times New Roman
by Newgen Publishing UK

I dedicate this book to
Angela Casey
Healer and Therapist
A very special and skilled person

Contents

About the Author

Dr Sue Jennings is a Professor of Play, a lifetime award from the European Federation of Dramatherapists. She is Senior Research Fellow of the Shakespeare Institute at the University of Birmingham, UK, a Distinguished Scholar at the University of the Witwatersrand, South Africa, and an Honorary Fellow of the University of Roehampton, London. She has previously held academic posts at the universities of Coleraine in Northern Ireland and Leeds Beckett, Derby, York St John, Roehampton, and Hertfordshire in England, is an Adjunct Professor at New York University, and a Visiting Professor at HELP University, Kuala Lumpur, Malaysia.

Her doctoral fieldwork was with the Temiars, a tribal people who live in the Malaysian rainforest. This research has been her greatest influence on the development and establishment of Neuro-Dramatic-Play, and has had a profound impact on all her educational and therapeutic work. It was there she realised that a society could have its own integrated system of both preventative and curative arts, including drama, dance, and music.

The other major influence in her life and work is Shakespeare and his plays and poetry. Her research at Stratford-upon-Avon, her school work in Education and Shakespeare, and her own performances have enriched her understanding of imagery, poetry, rhythm, and metaphor. She performed *The Nurse's Tale* at the Edinburgh Fringe and on tour throughout the UK.

Sue is responsible for establishing the British Association of Dramatherapists, an endeavour she later shared with fellow pioneer Gordon Wiseman. Together, they created many projects and training programmes in the UK and in Holland, Germany, and Greece. She has also innovated the training and practice of Dramatherapy and the Playtherapy Method in the UK, Malaysia, Romania, Korea, Greece, and Turkey.

Her publications include over 50 books on different aspects of dramatherapy and play therapy, Neuro-Dramatic-Play, Embodiment-Projection-Role, resilience, attachment, social and emotional intelligence, self-harming, trauma, dementia, depression, and play.

Sue co-edited with Dr Clive Holmwood *The Routledge International Handbook on Dramatherapy* (2016), which won an academic award, *The Routledge International Handbook of Play, Therapeutic Play and Play Therapy* (2020), and *The Routledge International Handbook of Therapeutic Stories and Storytelling* (2022).

Also for Routledge, she is currently compiling her selected works, *'Thither and Back Again': Journeys from Chaos to Order*. Recently, Sue has established herself as a children's author with a series of books for young children about Moose and Mouse.

Sue lives in Weston-Super-Mare, Somerset, UK, and enjoys playing with her young grandchildren. Her new interests are researching Vodnik stories and collecting antique marionettes.

Foreword

Even before the pandemic of 2020, anxiety was on the rise amongst children and young people as well as the wider population. Over the last few decades, young people in particular have been placed under increasing stress and anxiety with the rise of the internet and social media and the expectation to get more and more likes, to have the right body image, or feeling that they don't fit it. There is, however, greater acceptance of differences in sexuality and gender, which is positive, but none of this comes without acknowledging the anxieties it causes for children, young people, and parents.

In education, there are greater expectations on young people due to a combination of governmental, societal, and parental expectations. Over the last 30 years, the education system in the UK appears to have placed greater priorities on children's individual attainments and their impact upon each school's league ranking, and the school's place nationally – all influenced by government legislation with much less emphasis on things like play, which are no longer seen as a priority (Owen 2021). There is much less emphasis in education upon the arts, dance, drama, music, art making, play, and storytelling. These are essential for children of all ages. Why? They alleviate stress and anxiety as they have a much more embodied approach to children and young people's overall development – a bottom-up (body) and not a top-down approach (brain/body). If unsupported, social anxiety has the potential to lead to much more serious mental health issues where sparse, highly specialist resources may need to be drawn upon, along with the long waiting lists that go with these, especially in the UK health system.

What Sue Jennings presents us with here in this wonderful and unique new book is a much more embodied approach to societal anxiety for children and young people. There is a much greater focus on simple things like breathing – we have forgotten how to breathe and forgotten how to harness the power of our imagination and connect it to the rest of our body for positive change. Although there has been much research and development in arts in health in recent years (Daykin 2020), ironically this has not filtered down to or embedded itself in schools – if only arts for health were used more in schools! Recent ideas such as Polyvagal Theory (Porges 2011) have shown us that the body is connected through nerves and sinews in a complex way, and that it is not just the brain, but the brain–body connection which is important.

Sue Jennings has developed her ideas around social anxiety in this gem of a creative and resourceful book drawing together theories developed over a 50-year career, using such things as Neuro-Dramatic-Play (NDP, Jennings 2010) and her development of play therapy and dramatherapy theories and practice. Sue won't mind my saying that many of these ideas are not necessarily new, but forgotten – forgotten knowledge she first learned about as an anthropologist living with the Temiar people in the jungles of Malaysia (Jennings 1995). The Temiars were so connected with their environment that it taught them how to 'be' with their environment and with each other – something most of us have sadly lost in the hectic day-to-day life of modern western society, which ironically is rich in things we want, yet poor in the things we need, such as connection with our bodies and each other. This is a possible root cause of social anxiety, amplified by the COVID pandemic, which isolated so many young people away from their peers and created a frightening world in which they had to shut themselves away from an unseen virus that could kill!

This book is very timely, and welcome. It is divided into four parts, preceded by a clear introduction as to exactly what social anxiety is and its impact upon our children and young people. The introduction clearly explains Sue's theoretical paradigm, Neuro-Dramatic-Play, and attachment theory, which are at the centre of the approaches in this book.

Part I goes on to explain the importance of things given so little attention, such as nesting – places where young people feel safe and rooted, be that in school or home or other special places. As mentioned earlier, breathing is such a basic but essential aid to our management of anxiety, and it is central throughout this book. Sleep is also focused upon as being essential. All of this is explored through a series of exercises/activities and resources for busy teachers, mentors, support staff, carers, and therapists to use within the context of their work.

Part II follows with another wide range of activities, beginning with the idea of feeling safe, focusing on individual anxiety and the impact of how we perceive others' faces, and what a 'safe' place is really like for a young person. Part III considers the replacement of anxiety with energy, the use of ancient Mandalas to help to reveal modern truths, and the importance of stories – something I strongly agree with, as Sue and I recently released a book on the importance of the therapeutic use of stories (Holmwood, Jennings, and Jacksties 2022). Part IV offers a range of resources and worksheets referred to throughout this book which allow children and young people to really embody these ideas more fully and provide the busy professional with a rich resource of ideas to develop in the classroom or therapy room.

Finally, wherever these resources are used by a wide range of professionals, the idea of connecting the brain to the body through the imagination is central and essential to this work. Sue has always described NDP as being preventative, and this book is very much about preventing any form of social anxiety from getting any worse. If we can work with children and young people as soon as these issues start to emerge, we have the potential to enable them to work with their anxieties and allow them to produce changes for themselves that will help them to develop and cope with the world they live in. This world will not become any easier any time soon, in fact it will probably become more challenging, so what we need to do is equip children with the ability to cope and to manage in it so that they can begin to thrive in uncertain times in an uncertain world.

I wholly recommend this book and all its resources to the professionals who may choose to use it. It is full of all the essential and simple things we neglect in society, such as breathing, finding a safe place, and sleeping peacefully. It has taken Sue Jennings a lifetime to hone these ideas, to bring us back to basics, and to connect us with the most important thing we need to cope with in life – ourselves.

Dr Clive Holmwood, Associate Professor, Discipline of Therapeutic Arts, University of Derby

Acknowledgements

Huge thanks to George Johnson for last-minute editing and ideas for the original manuscript. I really appreciate the artwork created by Iain Macleod-Jones, as well as his editorial help with the final text. Thanks, too, to Sheng Ming Lau, who created much of the artwork for the worksheets.

My family and friends, especially those in Malaysia and Romania, have provided a lot of sustenance and support for me during these difficult times. Many thanks to Ming Yang for last-minute proofreading, and special thanks to Neil Johnson for the final ordering, checking, tidying, amendments, and rearrangement of the manuscript.

Finally, to Clive Holmwood, who has been a constant source of support – thank you.

Language: Cisgender, Trans, and Inclusivity

In her book *What's the T?*, Juno Dawson (2021) clarifies the current issues regarding LGBTQ+ and Trans and non-binary. For young people who are worried about their sexual and gender identities, there is support and understanding, both in the recent literature as well as the advisory and medical resources.

The World Health Organization (WHO n.d.) defines sex as:

> the different biological and physiological characteristics of females, males and intersex persons.

It defines gender as:

> the characteristics of women, men, girls and boys that are *socially constructed*. This includes norms, behaviours and roles associated with being a woman, man, girl or boy.

I have set the phrase 'socially constructed' in italics since it means that societies across the world define what it means to behave as male or female, and it is subject to change, whereas sex refers to the *biological and physiological* characteristics.

To give an example: in Victorian times, middle- and upper-class girl and boy children were dressed the same, in dresses and with long hair. The prevailing belief was that boy children might be stolen. At the age of 7, boy children went through a special ritual conducted by the father when the child's hair was cut and he wore his first pair of breeches, thus becoming a male child – a clear example of social construction of gender!

The history of gender across cultures is a fascinating subject studied by anthropologists and others, but what concerns us here are anxiety, identity, and gender dysphoria. Do look at the advice in Juno Dawson's book, which has information about helplines across several cultures, as well as sensible advice for parents. This book gives practical approaches to working with the anxiety so that issues and decisions about life changes can be made with reflection and insight.

COVID-19 and Anxiety

COVID anxiety has been increasing during the past two years. It is in families, small children, as well as young people, and indeed in most adults. Many people are worried for others, relatives, and neighbours, fearing that they might become ill or die. Others are worried for themselves: about dying, incapacity, or weakness. Would their jobs still be available after recovery? Professional people worry about their patients and whether they will recover. How do they prioritise diminishing resources amongst their patients? So much of this anxiety is about uncertainty and fear.

Unfortunately, all the advice from governments and clinics has reinforced the alienation we feel from other people: social distancing, masks, lack of socialising, rules of six, and more. Nevertheless, it is a good thing that we were encouraged to meet and socialise outdoors. Perhaps that could become a positive spin-off from the pandemic.

However, it is important to be aware that COVID anxiety is based on facts – a real disease that varies in its seriousness, and real anxiety about something real. This makes it very different from other types of anxiety such as agoraphobia, which is not usually based on real events.

The methods outlined in this book can be applied with all types of groups and with individuals, because all of them are empowering. They enable people to reflect on their anxiety and to make informed decisions. This book does not set out to provide a treatise about causes. It gives a methodology to improve personal strengths and reflective skills.

Introduction

The journey to discover this book in me has taken a long time. Being raised in an anxious family, I became an anxious adult, and spent much energy trying to disguise it. It was my own anxiety that led me to eventually try and find a means of changing it! Life was exhausting, and I spent a lot of time falling asleep in classes, on buses, and at the library. Psychoanalysis did not change this – if anything, it made me more anxious, and I needed a lot of theatre visits to experience a feeling of 'family in a house'.

However, when I was living with my children in the rainforest, I slept very deeply, my days were calmer, and this was despite the fact we were in a rather more dangerous environment! One contributory factor was the lack of competitiveness, both in child-rearing and between adults. There was an ethos of sharing resources and supporting each other in a hostile landscape. The Temiar believed that the greatest insult you could direct at someone was to call them mean. This meant that you did not share your resources adequately. For example, if you had two cigarettes left, they might ask you for one! When we returned to the UK, my younger son said, 'People are so grabby in England!'

It was highly significant that I became adopted into a family within a couple of weeks of arrival in the Temiar village where we were to live for almost 18 months. The senior village midwife, who lived with her adult children and their children in the same village, came to me one morning and said that I was her daughter. My children and I were now connected to this enormous family network, and we felt safe and welcome.

My love of Shakespeare started with my very first visit to Stratford-upon-Avon, soaking myself in the history and the atmosphere, in between visits to the theatre. Losing oneself in a play was the best antidote to anxiety and stress. It was a temporary relief as I had no mentor to manage the experience, but it gave me some clues. *A Midsummer Night's Dream* became my focus for in-depth research, and I realised that the four groups of people – lovers, the court, craftspeople, and the fairy world – could represent four aspects of the individual person! Could they co-exist? Or would they always be in conflict?

I was a strong pioneer in the original Dramatherapy movement, and director of two of the early training programmes. For me, it was linked to theatre and a means of understanding self and society through theatre. However, everything changed when the Arts Therapies became institutionalised through state registration and adopted a psychotherapeutic/psychoanalytic model. Even the timing of sessions followed the 50-minute/1½-hour model. Most of the Arts Therapies have become Arts Psychotherapies. Interestingly, Dramatherapy has not joined the psych focus; we must never forget that actors were considered no more than vagabonds for hundreds of years and therefore outside the mainstream. My main innovation for training people in Dramatherapy, as well as being theatre-focused, was the inclusion of Social Anthropology. I believed this brought about far greater cross-cultural understanding and a wider lens through which to understand the culture and creativity of groups and societies. I could not adhere to the primacy of the individual as demonstrated in psychotherapy and psychoanalysis. It was hugely relevant when neuroscientists announced the discovery of the roles of the right and left hemispheres of the brain. They described, amongst other attributes, how the left is concerned with facts, logic, numeracy, and the individual; the right is for the arts, intuition, feelings, metaphor, and groups.

My interest began to focus on pregnancy and childbirth, and when attachment might have the greatest impact. There is little written on pre-birth attachment, and most authorities talk about it developing towards the end of the first year. However, having been involved in many births in Malaysia when my Temiar mother asked me to be her assistant, I was particularly interested in life immediately after birth. The first few hours after birth is the time when the newborn tries to interact with their mother. The infant tries to imitate the mother's expression, and if she is not too exhausted, she will imitate back. This imitative interaction is the first step into a dramatised relationship, a performative theatrical beginning of an infant's identity through interaction. This led me to propose that civilisation is founded on theatre rather than language.

DOI: 10.4324/9781032256641-1

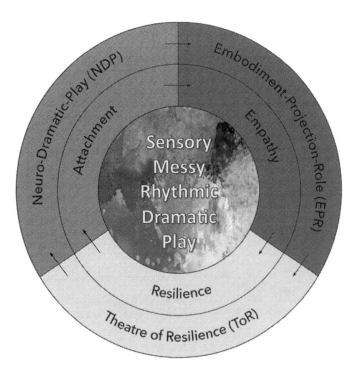

Figure 1 The Mandala for NDP, EPR, and ToR

This pivotal moment of childbirth seemed to be the consolidation of the attachment that developed during growth in the womb and the start of independent life, at least separate from the birth mother, although needing constant care and nurture. The infant's need to be held reinforces safety and security, and this need is present throughout life (Porges 2017; Dana 2021). Stephen Porges, who founded Polyvagal Theory, has promoted a deep understanding of our primary need to feel safe and how much behaviour can be understood as a demonstration of not feeling safe.

In concentrating on six months before and after birth and the major transition of the birth itself, I was able to focus on Neuro-Dramatic-Play (NDP), the precursor to Embodiment-Projection-Role (EPR), the developmental paradigm that charts the infant's growth from birth to 6 years. It overlaps with NDP during the first six months. Whereas the original 'embodiment' stage includes all whole-body movement as well as legs and arms, feet and hands, head and shoulders, tummy and bottom, it neglected sensory experience with all the senses, including touch. This was made good with NDP, where the four elements of sensory, messy, rhythmic, and dramatic play show the importance of the senses in developmental play, and NDP/EPR in particular. It was a while later that I realised dramatic play and role play have a performative element that consolidates around the age of 7 years. Therefore, the transition from EPR to Theatre of Resilience (ToR) integrates all the previous stages, and integrates drama and theatre as the performative basis of creative living.

In broad terms, NDP establishes attachment – EPR is a basis for developing empathy, and ToR allows the development of resilience.

There is growing concern that a generation of children are growing up incapable of expressing empathy – that is, understanding how another person feels. When mothers and babies imitate each other and exchange roles, they are expressing how the other person feels, so learning about empathy starts very early in life and needs adults to be able to tune into the baby's communication.

The Theory Underlying These Ideas: Love, Kindness, and Curiosity

An understanding of NDP and attachment-based play as a whole, specifically applied to social anxiety, forms the basis of the approach in this book. It also includes the understanding of transitions and change, which can be helped through playfulness. Attachment stories are included that can be applied in NDP practice which reflect 'love, kindness, and curiosity'.

Attachment and Pregnancy: The Circle and the Nest

Before a baby is born, it is contained within the circle of the womb. Floating in warm, slimy water, we need to remember the baby's first experience is in the dark. Attachment is growing during the pregnancy, and many mothers will start to be more playful. They talk to their unborn child, and will answer themselves 'as if' they are the baby. However, for some mothers it is a time of anxiety, especially if it is their first child. There may be fears of the birth itself, and worry about handing over control to others. A book I very strongly recommend is *The Positive Birth Book*, by Milli Hill (2017), which has become a best-seller. Milli talks us through all the basics and how to stay in control of one's own birth experience. The developmental stages of pregnancy are described in Jennings (2010, pp.85–87). It is crucially important that we keep mothers stress-free during pregnancy. Remember that the stress hormone, cortisol, can penetrate the placenta wall. We now know that for many individuals, their stress actually starts before they are born. Unborn infants can sense conflict in the outside world, and since the womb acts like an amplifier, they are very aware of raised voices. Rocking songs and gentle massage can all help to de-stress mothers-to-be. And remember that many pregnant women feel very lonely, and are quite overwhelmed when the baby is born. Think about what you can do to help, even if it means just taking the newborn for a little walk around the garden. There is now an increased awareness of the role of Doulas, who care for and support mothers after childbirth.

Circles of Attachment

Within a circle, we usually feel safe, especially if we can touch the edges. There are three circles of attachment for the small infant:

1. circle in the womb
2. circle in mother's arms
3. circle in mother's consciousness – intuitive awareness

Spontaneously, we hug or clasp or hold people in a circle when we greet, meet, or comfort. One of the cruelties of COVID-19 is that hugging was not allowed, even for older people who were very dependent. And occasional hugging in a mask, plastic apron, and gloves was scarcely a substitute.

Paediatricians, nurses, and other clinicians now realise that physical contact with premature babies actually helps their growth and development. Hands can now gently touch and stroke through holes in the incubator. Together with the gentle voice telling a story, this soothing touch is very important.

The circle is like a nest, and children's beds can be nest-like, with pillow and quilt. Even a small infant wearing a Babygro needs an additional blanket to create containment and 'safety in space'.

We dance in circles, make art on round plates, play games in circles.

Children love circular playing:

- spinning tops
- roundabouts and merry-go-rounds
- skipping and counting chants
- spinning until dizzy – either individually or in a group
- traditional circular playground games with actions and songs – Poor Jenny Sits a-Weeping, The Farmer's in His Den, Ring-a-Ring o' Roses (though you may need to modify some of the words)

Think about King Arthur and the Knights of the Round Table. Ancient theatre was 'in the round', as were many rituals and celebrations. Maybe consider afresh the idea of teaching and learning in the round – especially when playing outdoors. When we work or play in a circle, everyone can see each other and there is less feeling of hierarchy. Lines can mean that people are overlooked, and maybe unseen. In a circle, everyone can greet and acknowledge each other.

Neuro-Dramatic-Play: Establishing Attachment, Safety, and Curiosity

Rhythmic Play

We have a natural response to move in a rhythmic way, whether marching, skipping, or dancing. It is difficult to move against a rhythm – just as it is hard to intentionally sing out of tune.

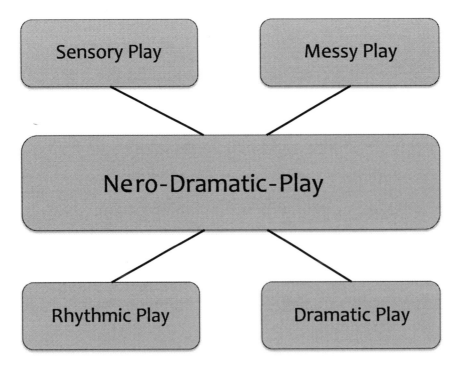

Figure 2 Neuro-Dramatic-Play

Mothers and babies spontaneously rock together, helped in the olden days with rocking chairs and cradles. Rocking is soothing and predictable, originating in the womb when a baby feels rocked in water when the mother moves.

The heartbeat is the first rhythmic experience, and creates security and repetition. Newborn babies will sometimes attune their own heartbeats to the heartbeats of their mothers. The regular heartbeat and the rocking, and also the movement when babies are carried in slings or back-frames, give a feeling of security, both through the physical touch as well as the regular rhythm.

Nursery rhymes, action songs, and poetry are all rhythmic forms that we can speak, sing, and dance to – if you need to learn a poem, try reciting it while you move in a rhythm. Remember the film *Renaissance Man*, when Danny DeVito had the soldiers learning Shakespeare speeches while marching!

Kelly Hunter points out that Shakespeare's verse mirrors the human heartbeat, which is why she uses it with children and teenagers on the autistic spectrum. Her application and exercises are described in her ground-breaking book *Shakespeare's Heartbeat* (Hunter 2014).

Sensory Play

There are many forms of sensory play that are important to include in early childhood experience. The development of our sensory system is crucial for our 'sense of self in space'. Too much cleaning and wiping, especially with artificial cleaners, can destroy our innate sensitivity, which needs careful stimulus. Many laundry products have harsh perfumes and textures, and clothes and bedding can become rough or prickly.

- Small babies need a soft touch, warmth, smoothness, gentle sounds, dim lights, and warm water and milk (breast if possible).
- Gradually introduce more sensory variations after a few months.
- Remember that even winter sunlight can be too harsh, so shaded light or sunglasses may be essential.
- Soon an infant will take interest in more variation in singing and rhythm, and will enjoy clapping and finger games.
- Whereas initially smooth food is preferred, different textures and colours can be introduced gradually.
- Crunchy carrots, apples, and cucumber can be enjoyed once there is no risk of choking and there are some teeth!
- Children will always return to milk and bottles when insecure or anxious: warm water and milk, rather than juice.
- A soothed baby will overall be able to cope with anxiety better than a nervous infant.

Messy Play: Familiarity and Exploration

From the warm waters of the womb, babies are born in a lot of mess. They are sticky and slimy, and often need holding firmly. Fortunately, doctors and nurses are more enlightened these days, and place the baby directly on the mother's chest rather than immediately washing and weighing. The cleaning up process is gradual, both for mother and baby, but the mess usually continues during feeding, with dribbling and spills, and can be enhanced with splashing and bubbles at bath time. Messy play and water play are known experiences for the infant which started before birth, but messy play can also spark curiosity as the infant realises that there are different colours or textures, or that water has different temperatures, or that bubbles can burst or float.

The balance between familiarity and exploration needs to be fine-tuned, and small infants who experience sudden change can become anxious. Some infants will hold onto sameness when changes have been too sudden, or they may develop a stimulus for change and bring about new experiences, one after the other. Both can be symptoms of anxiety that can become embedded and slow to change.

Ideally, mess leads to exploration leads to form, or chaos through experiment becomes order.

Dramatic (or Interactive) Play

Sensory, messy, and rhythmic play do not happen sequentially, but are intertwined during early development, both pre- and post-birth, and continue in some shape or form throughout life.

It is the same with dramatic play, which emerges when mothers are dramatically playful with their unborn child, telling stories and recounting events, and having conversations, answering themselves as if they are the child. A beautiful example of this is in *Under Milk Wood* by Dylan Thomas, when Polly Garter is talking to her new-born baby:

> Me, Polly Garter, under the washing line, giving the breast in the garden to my bonny new baby. Nothing grows in our garden, only washing. And babies. And where's their fathers live, my love? Over the hills and far away. You're looking up at me now. I know what you're thinking, you poor little milky creature. You're thinking, you're no better than you should be, Polly, and that's good enough for me. Oh, isn't life a terrible thing, thank God?"

(Thomas 1954/2015, p.24)

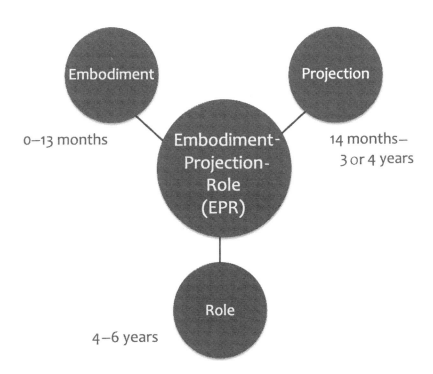

Figure 3 Embodiment-Projection-Role

The poet has a remarkable insight into the early life of the infant. Mothers and babies are interactive within hours of birth, when babies try to imitate the expression on their mother's face. This very early imitation continues the infant's 'dramatic development' and enables different roles to emerge.

Neuro-Dramatic-Play is the overarching paradigm that charts development through to the end of life. However, it also refers to the first stage of development, six months before and after birth, leading into and overlapping with Embodiment-Projection-Role.

Embodiment-Projection-Role

By understanding Embodiment-Projection-Role, practitioners and parents have a learning grid through which they can observe the learning stages of the small child (aged 14 months–6 years) and also introduce the re-learning stages when there has been a developmental delay.

Embodiment-Projection-Role is a developmental paradigm that has been growing in application and understanding since the 1980s. It is used in clinical and educational practice as well as in research and child observation. EPR also forms the basis of various training programmes in arts and play therapies and in early years practice. The three stages and their transitions are necessary for healthy physical, neurological, and emotional development. I have continued to develop and refine EPR. The more recent NDP paradigm is a detailed refinement of the Embodiment stage, and commences earlier, from conception rather than birth. EPR sits neatly between NDP and Theatre of Resilience (which starts at around 6 years):

- *Embodiment* – birth–12 or 13 months: Everything is through the body: whole-body movement, limb movement, sensory experience, chanting and repetition, breathing, and sound.
- Transition: A special toy or blanket becomes the infant's first symbol (made famous by Winnicott (1971/ 1991/1995) and 'the transitional object'.
- *Projection* – 14 months–3 or 4 years: Although the infant is still very physical, the focus is on life beyond the body. Fired by curiosity as well as manipulation and coordination, infants play with mess, finger paints, puzzles (What fits where?). Projective play becomes more complex, with increased interest in stories and family scenes in the doll's house and playing with puppets.
- Transition: An increased use of a special object, such as a magic wand or a hat or cap, points the way towards the Role stage.
- *Role* – 3 or 4 years–6 years: Increasingly, small children experiment and create roles, sometimes telling a story and playing all the roles as well as the narrator. As they approach 6 years, there is a growing sense of a role being 'right', such as 'Daddies don't talk like that' or 'The Grandma walks with a stick.'

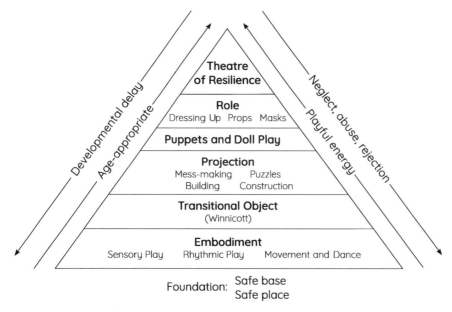

Figure 4 The EPR Triangle

Role Stages

In the following role stages, we can see how there is an urge to play dramatically from birth, and this consolidates by the age of 6 or so. For anxious children, it can be, later as they will often hold onto their anxious role until they feel safe:

1. The dramatic response, or 'as if' – this starts shortly after birth when the infant and mother imitate each other.
2. 'My body–your body' – whole-body play takes place between adult and infant (and later becomes rough-and-tumble play), including moving up and down, flying, and knee bouncing, sometimes with rhymes.
3. 'Peep-bo!' – the adult puts their hands over their face, and then 'appears' again, and the infant enjoys the repetition and feeling of excitement. The delay in appearance can be slowly increased: for small infants, when you have gone, you are gone.
4. 'Role reversal' – a child talks to special toy and then answers 'as if' they are the toy. This mirrors what has taken place between mother and unborn child, and in the early stages after birth.
5. 'Ordering and re-ordering' – soft toys or farm or wild animals are lined up and assigned roles. They often interact, and are given voices and feelings, assigned as goodies and baddies, good or naughty.
6. 'Creating narratives' – whereas earlier play had the elements of narrative, children now combine elements together into a story structure. It may be on an epic scale, or a very simple conversation and an outcome.
7. 'Improvisation and story' – children can spend an appreciable amount of time improvising a story or idea or scene. It may lead to a performance that shows an understanding of aesthetics and structure.

Usually, stages 1–3 are achieved by 6 months, stages 4 and 5 by 3 years, and 6 and 7 by 6 years-plus (Jennings 2017a). There is a performative element running through all the stages from birth which becomes crystallised in the final stage. Then it is time to move forward into the performative paradigm, Theatre of Resilience (ToR).

Theatre of Resilience

As children spend increased time playing out different roles in stories and plays and putting on performances for families and friends, there is an increase both in confidence and independence. Children who are anxious find role play and drama difficult, and will often avoid situations that provoke uncertainty. Although most children will easily move into performances, the anxious child is more likely to stay with an embodied or projective activity. Drama can feel nebulous or without boundaries, and the anxious child needs certainties.

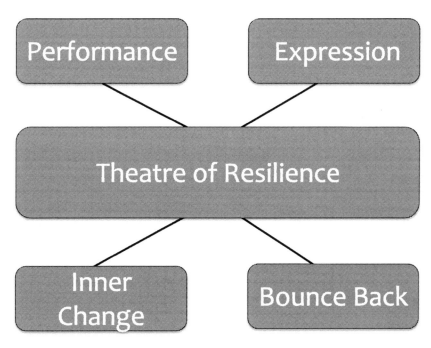

Figure 5 Theatre of Resilience

Theatre of Resilience works from the outside in – exploring the emotions of a character makes an impact and change on the inner life, which enables the person to bounce back. By exploring the feelings of the character, the individual's inner life is kept intact until they feel confident to come closer.

Performance needs to be encouraged as a participatory subject rather than an opportunity to show off to indulgent parents!

Attachment Story Chant

This story is an example of attachment-based play which illustrates an EPR approach. It features repetition and sequencing, and can be used with all infants and young children. Children can learn the words as well as make movements, for example the big eyes and the big mouth. The chant and ideas could also be given to parents. It is an action chant that mothers can do during pregnancy and early months after birth.

The Tadpoles Are Looking for Mummy (from China)

A group of tadpoles live in a pond happily. One day, one of the tadpoles says:

> 'Everyone has a mummy, but who is our mummy?
> Yes, who is our mummy?
> I want a mummy
> I miss mummy
> Why not look for our mummy?
> Good idea! Let's go!'

They are swimming around.
Then they meet a duck.

> 'Is she our mummy?
> Are you our mummy?'
> 'No, I'm not your mummy.
> I'm a duck. I am duckling's mummy.'
> 'Do you know who our mummy is?
> What does she look like?'
> 'Your mummy's name is Frog
> She has two big eyes and a big mouth.'
> 'Thank you, thank you,
> We are going to look for our mummy.
> See you later.'
> 'Good luck!'

They are swimming around.
Then they meet a fish.

> 'She has two big eyes and a big mouth.
> Is she our mummy?
> Are you our mummy?'
> 'No, I'm not your mummy. I'm a fish.
> I am little fish's mummy.'
> 'Do you know who our mummy is?
> What does she look like?'
> 'Your mummy's name is Frog,
> Your mummy has two big eyes
> A big mouth, and a big white stomach.'
> 'Thank you, thank you,
> We are going to look for our mummy,
> See you later!'
> 'Good luck.'

They are swimming around.
Then they meet a crab.

   'She has two big eyes, a big mouth,
   And a big white stomach.
   Is she our mummy?
   Are you our mummy?'
   'No, I'm not your mummy. I'm a crab.
   I'm little crab's mummy.'
   'Do you know who our mummy is?
   What does she look like?'
   'Your mummy's name is Frog.
   Your mummy has two big eyes, a big mouth
   And a big white stomach and four legs.'
   'Thank you, thank you!
   We're going to look for our mummy,
   See you later!'
   'Good Luck!'

They are swimming around.
Then they meet a tortoise.

   'She has two big eyes and a big mouth,
   A big white stomach and four legs.
   Is she our mummy?
   Are you our mummy?'
   'No, I'm not your mummy, I'm a tortoise.
   I'm little tortoise' mummy.'
   'Do you know who our mummy is?
   What does she look like?'
   'Your mummy's name is Frog
   Your mummy has two big eyes, a big mouth,
   A big white stomach, four legs, and a green back.'
   Thank you, thank you!
   We are going to look for our mummy,
   See you later.'
   'Good luck.'

They go on swimming.
At this time, a frog approaches.

   'She has two big eyes and a big mouth,
   A big white stomach, four legs, and a green back.
   Are you our mummy?'
   'Sure, my dear babies. Come on!'
   'Mummy! Mummy!
   We have a Mummy!
   Mummy, I love you!'

There is extensive learning from this delightful story-chant. For younger children, there is recognition of colours and animals, naming animals, repetition, and sequencing; for older children, all of the stated learning, plus understanding how one can recognise something or someone by giving greater detail. For all children, there is the theme of attachment. Some of the language would need to be adapted when working with looked-after children; inserting the word 'special' will often be enough.

Practical Exercises

Ascertain the child's/children's level of knowledge regarding the animals. It may be necessary to show pictures and talk about the animals without being over-directive. Usually, the following exercises would be developed after the reading of the story-chant:

1. Move around the room as tadpoles swim. Remember in the story it said that they swam 'around'. Swim a bit faster, and then slower. – *Embodiment*
2. Now move around the room like the fish swimming. How are the tadpoles and fish different in the way they swim? Don't tell me – show me! –*Embodiment*
3. Choose one animal to draw and colour: both the mummy and the babies. –*Projection*
4. Create a collage showing the mothers and babies and water and plants. –*Projection*
5. Move around like a crab. Show your pincers snapping! Are you in water or on the land? – *Beginning of Role*
6. Let's change to a land creature. Move around the room as a tortoise, with four legs. You hear a sound! Now stop and protect your head and legs with your shell. Look out of your shell. All is safe, so continue your walk. – *Role and the beginning of the story*
7. You may choose to introduce the idea of the 'safe place' here, using the example of the tortoise. – *Drama for specific learning*

Developmental Outdoor Play

The more children can play out of doors, the healthier the development of both body and brain. Young children need outdoor play for on average four hours per day. Even in cold or wet weather, there are great advantages to playing in nature and away from screens. Puddle jumping, stream splashing (under supervision of course!), and 'rain catching' are all important ways of water play.

Sensory play excites the senses of touch, smell, sounds, taste, and sight, and may include:

- the feel of wet mud and water
- the smell of wet grass, old tree bark, and flowers
- the sound of bird calls, insects scratching, and water splashing
- the taste of wild fruit such as blackberries
- the sight of rainbows, insects, and birds' nests

Who Is This Book For?

This book is written for teachers and therapists, care workers, teaching assistants, parents, and all those involved in the support and development of children and young people. It provides an introduction to theory and a range of techniques from both a creative perspective as well as a CBT approach. Different approaches will appeal to different individuals and groups, and your methods can vary depending on the context. However, the main thrust of this way of working is to always consider the need for *nurture and nesting*, and the necessity of *safety*.

The book gives ideas and applications for those who have become locked in social anxiety. This often contributes to their lack of motivation in life and learning. In my book *101 Ideas for Increasing Focus & Motivation* (Jennings 2015), I build on a theme of change from core negativity to core positivity. One of the reasons why people avoid learning is the anxiety that is blocking their pathways, and that applies to any age group. It is important to remember that COVID-19 also had an enormous impact on the lives of individuals and families, and the ensuing anxiety increased, both regarding the disease itself as well as the major changes in lifestyle.

This book is also written for children and young people themselves, and suggests ways their fears and anxieties can be challenged and changed. They can look up exercises and choose one they would like to work on, whether working individually or in a group. Allowing them to choose encourages their autonomy, and may be the first step in anxiety reduction. If working in a group, then participants can take turns each week to choose an exercise for the group. They can also have the opportunity to talk about their choices. The main focus is on the age range 9–15 years, although most techniques can be adapted for younger children and older teens.

The book is divided into four parts. Each part includes theory, creative exercises, CBT techniques, case examples, and a discussion.

Part I, 'Breathing, Sleep, and Mindfulness', gives several examples of the basics of addressing social anxiety. Always be aware of breathing patterns and how they can be changed to reduce anxiety. Part II, 'Perceptions, Feelings, and Safety', focuses on how we see anxiety, and whether we can 're-draw' the scene.

Part III, 'Energy, Mandalas, and Stories', looks at the energy we lose while trying to maintain our anxiety, and various techniques that can be used to 're-energise' us to participate in educational and social activities we have been missing.

Part IV, 'Resources', includes worksheets, story sheets, and handouts for children and young people to take home.

Appendix 1 describes various de-stress physical exercises and drama games that can be used as starters and warm-ups. Appendix 2 is a short description of 'white noise' and the current debate about whether it aids small infants with sleeping.

It is important to remember that all the exercises can be modified to suit individual situations, and that where possible, children and young people should be empowered to choose activities that 'speak' to their experience.

What Is Social Anxiety?

Social anxiety is not always recognised until it becomes embedded in the person's lifestyle and management. The individual and people around them will often make excuses or try to conceal the fact that there are issues.

Social anxiety is the fear of interaction with other people that brings on self-consciousness, nervousness, and feelings of being negatively judged and evaluated, and as a result often leads to avoidance of anxiety-provoking situations. People with social anxiety feel they are being constantly negatively judged by other people, and this can lead to feelings of inadequacy, inferiority, embarrassment, humiliation, and depression.

Most people at some time in their lives experience anxiety, but they may in fact not actually be anxious, they may be shy. The two words are often confused. Many people are known as 'shy', which doesn't prevent them from interacting with others, but makes them a little more cautious, often waiting for a response from someone else before initiating communication themselves.

Literature is full of shy or introverted people who are often considered dull, such as Anne Elliot in Jane Austen's *Persuasion*, or lonely, like Aaliya Salah in Rabih Alameddine's *An Unnecessary Woman*, or rude, like Mr Darcy in Jane Austen's *Pride and Prejudice*. However, they display hidden depths in the end, and there are special people who do see their positive qualities. Bilbo Baggins in Tolkien's *Lord of the Rings* is a very good example of an introvert who prefers his own company, but who nevertheless can be brave and adventurous when called upon. He tells Gandalf that he feels 'thin, stretched out, like butter scraped over too much bread'.

We talk about 'shrinking violets', 'coming out of one's shell', 'our loudness is constrained in our brains', 'as timid as a rabbit', 'as shy as a mouse'. People who are shy, timid, or introverted are not in the true sense socially anxious. They are usually exercising a preference for their own company or the company of familiar people

However, a socially anxious young person may hide behind a family 'role', such as 'Jane's always been shy, just like her mother.' Anxious teenagers may be given labels by teachers or parents: for example, 'Sam is the introvert' or 'Polly has always been quiet.' And children can be smiled at when they 'hide behind mother's skirts' or succeed because 'they are such a hard worker, always in their bedrooms perfecting their homework'. This labelling avoids actually addressing the anxiety which can be the cause of enormous pain and suffering. A more contemporary example is when people say 'John is a little bit Aspie [Asperger's]' or 'Ignore Lizzie, she's having an autistic moment!' Both these statements are impossible, and confuse a developmental condition with anxiety states. Nevertheless, people with autism or Asperger's can also feel anxious.

Social anxiety usually affects people's interactions with the world around them far more seriously than shyness. People describe physical feelings of:

- increased heart rate
- sinking sensations in their stomach
- sweating and clamminess
- going hot and cold
- prickly feelings in their joints
- shaky knees
- frozen body – unable to move
- thumping bowel sensation
- needing to pee
- dizziness
- nausea

People may also have feelings of:

- dread
- panic

- fear
- humiliation
- self-criticism
- self-blame
- self-harm or suicide

These physical experiences and feelings result in certain behaviours, including avoidance of a situation (the classical fight, freeze, or flight) and various strategies to deal with anxiety-provoking situations.

Assessment for Social Anxiety

The UK National Institute for Health and Care Excellence (NICE) guidelines offer some useful pointers when we are assessing school-age children up to the age of 17. They offer a series of questions that can be asked with the person alone or with an accompanying adult.

Here are the guidelines:

- Provide an opportunity for the child or young person to be interviewed alone at some point, during the assessment.
- If possible, involve a parent, carer, or other adult known to the child or young person who can provide information about current and past behaviour.
- If necessary, involve more than one professional to ensure a comprehensive assessment can be undertaken.
- When assessing a child or young person, obtain a detailed description of their current social anxiety and associated problems, including feared and avoided social situations.
- Establish what they are afraid might happen in social situations (for example, looking anxious, blushing, sweating, trembling, or appearing bored).

Anxiety symptoms may be:

- negative view of self
- critical content of self-image
- safety-seeking behaviours
- avoiding being focus of attention in social situations

Useful information to gather includes:

- Are there friendships and peer groups?
- What are the educational and social circumstances?
- Is there medication, alcohol, or recreational drug use?
- As part of a comprehensive assessment, assess for causal and maintaining factors for social anxiety disorder in the child or young person's home, school, and social environment, in particular.
- Are there parenting behaviours that promote and support anxious behaviours or do not support positive behaviours?
- Is there peer victimisation in school or other settings?

Factors that contribute to lack of change include:

- lack of self-esteem and self-confidence
- worrying thoughts and anxieties
- disbelief in the possibilities of success
- avoidance of change and new situations

For more information regarding the NICE guidelines on social anxiety, go to www.nice.org.uk and click on 'Guidance'.

This approach is all very well, but in many situations we are working with children and young people who would find answering questions extremely anxiety-provoking. The formality of the interaction implies expectations, and that is often what provokes anxiety! The NICE guidelines could be used just like that – as guidelines. Many of the suggestions could be addressed by using creative techniques. For example, self-image could be explored through drawing a self-portrait, or anxious situations could be role-played.

Liana Lowenstein (2002) has a delightful ice-breaker for questions in her book *More Creative Interventions for Troubled Children and Youth*. She suggests having a bag of crisps, and the adult and young person/child taking it in turns to ask a question and take a crisp. What a creative and fun approach!

What I suggest in this book is that developing the core processes of breathing, rhythm, sound, and physical movement can lead to a reduction of anxiety and a new awareness of the self. I also illustrate how drama games are a positive way of developing social skills and group interaction. Drama games start very simply, so that no one is set up to fail.

Possible Causes and Indicators of Social Anxiety

It is important to remember that the physical, the emotional, and the behavioural all start with thinking. Many young people think that they don't look good, they are overweight, they are not going to succeed, they are going to fail. All of these negative thoughts manifest themselves through feelings in the body, in emotions, and in behaviour. If such thought processes are established in young years, then they are likely to continue into adult life, so it is important to address them as soon as possible.

Many of these negative thoughts have built up over time, and may come from critical comments from parents, teachers, and peers. It isn't helpful when parents compare their children and praise one more than another. These parental attitudes are fixed very early in a child's life, so that by the teenage years they have often come entrenched – for example, 'Why don't you be more like your sister? She knows what to do,' can become embedded as 'I'm not as good as others.' These types of comments can become established physically, so changing them seems like a major undertaking.

The following are some of the signs of social anxiety in children and young people, and parents and teachers should look out for behaviours that start to become habitual, such as:

- stopping going out
- thinking of what might go wrong in a future situation
- worrying about what others see and think of you
- suddenly becoming 'tongue-tied' and not knowing what to say
- avoiding social situations
- staying in places that feel safe
- avoiding having face-to-face contact with people

Some of the visible physical signs of social anxiety can be:

- bitten nails
- wearing hair falling in front of the face
- placing a hand over the mouth when speaking

Some children and young people may also change their style of dress so that they do not stand out. One of the most difficult things for them is to be noticed, and they are very embarrassed when people draw attention to them. Deliberately sitting at the back of the class or behind a taller person are ways of not being noticed.

Understanding the Anxious Brain

The destructive aspect of anxiety is that it makes a direct impact on the brain and undermines the higher-order thinking processes, so instead of being able to objectively weigh up decisions or critically evaluate a situation, thoughts become personalised. People with social anxiety are usually stuck in their 'instinctual brain'. This part of the brain is sometimes called 'reptilian' or 'reactive', and is necessary for survival. For example, we need this part of the brain to remind us to eat or drink, to find shelter, to keep warm. But in some situations, unhelpful messages can get into this brain area, so we will react adversely to seemingly harmless situations. For example, a person might not notice somebody standing near them, and that person might interpret that as being deliberately ignored. A teacher who addresses the whole class in an irritated manner may cause one person in the group to feel they are being attacked personally.

This new model of addressing issues of social anxiety is mainly based on the mammal brain and nurture. The mammalian or limbic brain is responsible for nurture, care, attachment and relationships, and being looked after. By taking a nurturing approach, we can establish a feeling of nurture and safety within which the social anxiety can be addressed.

Figure 6 The anxious brain

What we hope to encourage in addressing social anxiety is the development of that part of the brain known as the region of executive function or higher-order thought. This part of the brain allows us to make decisions, to reflect before we react, and to give time before taking action. Many young people will react without thinking as they do not have the capacity to wait before making a decision; with children and teenagers alike, this is often the result of feeling anxious. Instant results are more desirable than waiting, because if you have to wait, the outcome might be wrong. Many of the strategies used to entice young people into choosing fashion styles, food, or even body shapes are based on this concept of being reactive, rather than on reflection and choice. Advertising is very skilled at finding the hook for people to make instant decisions through phrases such as 'everybody must have this product', 'don't be seen without ...' and 'the whole world's talking about it'. As a result, this can feed feelings of anxiety and stress around social interactions and self-image.

In education, young people are being asked more frequently to make early decisions about their futures. They need to specialise at an early age when many of their ideas have not been formed. Consequently, they become anxious about their choices, submit to pressure about other people's decisions, or make decisions based on the expectations of their peers, teachers, and parents which can often lead to failure and depression.

We need, then, to be aware of the three important aspects of the brain: the reactive brain, the nurturing brain, and the decision-making brain. This will help us to make the right provision for children and young people locked into painful and anxious states of mind.

The Basis of This Book

In creating this book, I was aware of the potential for increased anxiety caused by the way the activities are set up for children and young people. I have throughout taken a 'nurturing model' in which young people can feel safe, or safer, in order to experiment with their anxiety. Each step of the way, the person can make a decision about whether to do something or not. The steps are small in order to encourage participation.

The nurturing part of the brain is linked to our early attachment experience, where in healthy development we are able to learn to trust other people. Eric Erikson (1965/1995), in his seminal book *Childhood and Society*, talks about the first major step in a child's life at 0–18 months, when either trust or mistrust is established. A child or young person with social anxiety mistrusts the world around them. For whatever reason, their early experience has not enabled them to trust the adults to provide predictability, constancy, and security.

One way of understanding social anxiety is to see that the individual is desperately trying to create an environment that is constant. So, by avoiding certain situations, the child or young person doesn't need to take any steps into the unknown. Parties, social get-togethers, family birthdays, and celebrations are the source of nightmares for many children and young people with social anxiety. They will avoid these social situations, often using repeated reasons, such as not feeling well, or making 'convenient' other plans. Furthermore, if certain days at school are particularly stressful as they involve particular lessons, sports, exams, or outings, they may develop a headache or stomach ache as a way of avoiding the situation. Physical symptoms associated with anxiety are real enough at the time, even though they may not have a basis in being unwell. Usually, the physical symptoms will disappear when the individual is feeling safe.

This Book Takes a Different Approach

The exercises in this book provide a template for approaching social anxiety with children and young people. Some individuals might prefer to work initially on a one-to-one basis, and perhaps join a group at a later stage, others might prefer to have the anonymity of a group rather than feeling exposed individually. Where possible, encourage everyone to choose how they would prefer to work.

Example

The setting was an anti-bullying conference, where adults could attend if invited by a young person. The authorities recommended that there should be counsellors available to provide one-to-one individual counselling if any young person became distressed. This was not what the young people wanted!
A group of Play Therapists and Dramatherapists set up a large table in the foyer, covered it with wallpaper, and provided a supply of crayons, coloured pens, and plasticine. It was announced on the tannoy that there was a graffiti table in the entrance hall.
It was a magnet!
Young people flocked to the table and wanted to draw, model, and talk: they expressed their distress and anxiety about being bullied, abused, and victimised. They felt secure with other young people around. When we provided masks, the young people found them a vehicle for expressing how they were feeling, and how at last people were listening to them.

The exercises in the nurture model start from a point of view identifying a place where people feel safe and cosy, taking the image of the nest. Participants are invited to explore where they feel safe and cosy. For many, it will be somewhere in their house, for others it might be in a private space outside, such as the shed or by the river, and so on. One might expect that most children or young people would choose their bedroom as the safe place, but be aware that in some instances their bedroom has not been safe owing to issues of abuse, or is a place they have been sent as a punishment.

When children or young people are isolated as a punishment and told to 'calm down', it is likely to increase their stress. This often follows a 'meltdown' or a trauma-associated episode. A likely initial response is flight – running away – or fight, or freeze – becoming immobile. If bedrooms are then used as a place of punishment, the likely outcome is that the associated stress will cause their brains to become flooded with the destructive chemical cortisol. These children and young people will also retain a negative association with their bedrooms that will be another cause of anxiety.

Places of safety become especially important for children and young people who are fostered or adopted. It is easy to assume that the looked-after child will feel safe in a new environment. This is frequently not the case. They will bring their feelings of mistrust and lack of safety with them into their new environment.

Many of the activities and exercises we use have direct relevance for the participants, and they can be given as worksheets to participants for use outside of the group sessions or at home. It can be helpful to encourage children and young people to choose the exercises they feel are right for them, so they have autonomy in their own healing process.

How to Use This Book

Before setting up individual or group interventions about social anxiety (Parts II and III), it may be advisable to work in a 'preventative' mode. For example, within lessons about personal and social issues, one could address issues that are fearful for children and young people (and others!). Whole projects could be planned on some of the following:

*   world events and headlines on TV or newspapers
*   death or loss of grandparents or parents
*   other people's opinion about looks, features or clothes

- expectations of parents or school
- personal safety including a possibility of abuse
- generalised 'What might happen if …?'
- my thoughts about vaccines
- home schooling in pandemics
- home education instead of school
- COVID-19 and its impact

Many children and young people take these issues in their stride, but many others have both specific fears as well as a sense of fear, all of which can turn into anxiety. The following example turned into a workshop that addressed some issues about social anxiety, although it was designated as a history project!

Example

I was running a drama workshop for 7–11-year-olds, on the theme of 'Pilgrimages' as part of a history project linked with the local abbey. We discussed reasons why people went on a pilgrimage, and the group members decided the following:

1. You had done something very wrong and wanted to say sorry.
2. You or someone you knew were ill and hoped for healing.
3. You were worried about something.

One 10-year-old came and said very quietly to me, 'My big sister has got her exams soon and I'm really worried about her. Can I bring that as a reason?'
It reminded me that pressures and expectations not only affect the individual, but can also impinge on other members of the family. This younger sibling was clearly affected by her big sister's anxiety, and she looked as if she was carrying the burden of worry. She looked very relieved once she had shared her concerns.
   Another boy said he was a murderer and wanted to say sorry. Partway through the project, he came to me and said, 'Miss – I'm not a murderer, I've broken my leg' – the flexibility of 'Let's pretend'!

The Nurturing Environment

Whether we are a participant or a facilitator, it is important that we can recognise whether an environment is nurturing, and a number of strategies can be used to help it feel more comfortable. An office or studio can have appropriate pictures on the walls: scenes of gardens, woodlands, a sea-shore. In the space can be soft, cuddly toys, cushions, small blankets. Chairs can be upholstered rather than plain wood. It is worthwhile finding out from children and young people what makes them feel relaxed and whether there are familiar objects they would like to see in the space. It is important to add here that some teachers and therapists (e.g., Moore 2021) work in people's homes in order to minimise the stress of coming to a new environment.

As part of your assessment, you can check out whether there is a calm environment or space at home. There are examples in Part IV, "Resources", that can be made into a handout for a child or young person to think about and see whether they can make some changes at home. Some of the techniques in this book involve bedtime routines, preparation for sleep, and so on, and the home handouts for these can be adapted or copied.

Equipment

As well as the décor, resources for the sessions can be sensory. For example, fabrics such as velvet, silk, and soft woven cotton feel soothing to the touch and something we might like to put around our shoulders and rub our cheeks on. Many clothes or fabrics can be bought at charity shops and then washed or dry-cleaned. Try not to use polyester, as it can cause sweating or irritation. The place where we feel nurtured mustn't feel sterile or cold. It needs to have all of the soft ingredients for us to feel looked after.

When you do the exercises in this book, try and keep these factors in mind when you try something new. Maybe you'll want to start wearing soothing clothes when you participate in anxiety reduction programmes. Whether you do it in reality or your imagination, throughout every exercise keep in mind the notion of nurturing touch. As teachers and therapists, we can wear nurturing clothing, encourage participants to imagine they are wearing something sensory, or suggest they wrap up in a shawl or blanket.

It's important to remember that we must not create more anxiety while trying to reduce existing anxiety!

By having an 'open book' approach to our work with children and young people, we are promoting a process of democracy where the participants will have a greater sense of being able to influence their day-to-day lives. This book has been written in developmental sequences, so it will be of benefit to commence with Part I, which covers the basics, especially bodywork and breathing. The approach is very much 'bottom-up' for our brains – starting with the reactive brain, followed by the nurturing brain, and finally the decision-making brain – rather than the conventional 'top-down' approach that starts with thinking rather than feeling.

Finally, on a personal note to this introduction, I would like to propose that we can all learn so much from the BBC programme *The Repair Shop* – a group of very skilled people who take joy in restoring people's personal treasures, and who all get on together! What a wonderful role model for business and family, for crisis and for politics!

Summary

This introduction has looked at the basis for understanding social anxiety and the 'official' guidelines for assessments. It discussed the question of a new model by looking at a lack of nurture as a way of approaching anxiety, and how we can try to replace it both through our techniques as well as the environment we create. Throughout, there has been an emphasis on empowering children and young people to make their own choices about how they would like to explore their feelings.

Part I

Breathing, Sleep, and Mindfulness

Introduction

There are three chapters in Part I of this book: 'Nesting and Breathing', 'Solutions for Sleep', and 'Sleep, Relaxation, and Light'. They include exercises to assist with stress reduction and to help develop new skills for breathing in order to alleviate anxiety. The main techniques covered are Creative Arts exercises, and each chapter ends with techniques that fall under Cognitive Behaviour Therapy (CBT).

The Creative Arts techniques are suitable for working with individuals or groups, and the main requirement is a calm ambience without interruptions. A room that people passing by cannot look into is important – you can cover windows if necessary and ensure that doors are closed. The resources for many of the exercises throughout the book include a blanket or shawl – participants can be invited to wrap themselves in these if they wish, to enhance feelings of security and comfort – and a floor mat, so that they can sit or lie down more comfortably.

Feeling Safe: Nurture and Nesting

The approach in this book is informed by Polyvagal Theory, invented by Stephen Porges , who maintains that safety is an intuitive and relevant aspect of people's lives (see Porges 2011 and 2017). He suggests that there is a 'top-down' emphasis in our society which gives greater importance to cognitive processes rather than bodily experiences.

Porges says:

> Parenting and educational strategies are targeted toward expanding and enhancing cognitive processes while inhibiting bodily feelings and impulses to move. The result is a *corticocentric* orientation in which there is a top-down bias emphasizing mental processes and minimizing the bottom-up feeling emanating from our body.
>
> (Porges 2017, p.33)

This is very much the focus of Neuro-Dramatic-Play: starting with the body and feeling safe in order to establish attachment.

Learning Outcomes for Part I

- understanding comfortable qualities and spaces
- developing awareness of breath waves and their control
- discovering techniques that encourage sleep
- practising mindfulness to focus on personal rhythms and heartbeats
- allowing relaxation where appropriate
- understanding hypervigilance
- feeling safe through 'nurture and nesting'

Creative Arts Techniques

You may wish to start with a discussion regarding anxiety, but in my own experience, young people have had their fill of being expected to talk about their feelings, and can often switch off.

One of the 'Warm-ups and Starters' in Appendix 1 can provide a good starting point before embarking on the exercises themselves. However, it is very important to ensure that young people are not set up to fail. One of the

DOI: 10.4324/9781032256641-2

greatest fears of socially anxious children and young people is that they are not good enough and will not make the grade. All of the exercises must be optional throughout, and participants should be encouraged to work at their own pace.

The ideas in this part are all connected with changing people's perceptions of themselves and helping them understand how they may tend to maintain levels of 'not succeeding' in order to justify their anxiety. Breathing is a means through which we can change self-perception.

Once participants are able to regulate their own breathing, then creativity can follow. The breathing rhythms can relax people and decrease anxiety, and can be helpful for sleeplessness. If we are able to synchronise the internal rhythms of heartbeat and pulse, we may be better able to connect with external rhythms through drumming or movement.

If you are working with a group, it is important to hold a preliminary session in order to focus on a learning agreement between everyone. In this first session, ideas can be illustrated and a group contract agreed upon – see Worksheet 1: Group Contract (page 104). People will feel more comfortable if they have some understanding of what the sessions are going to involve.

Worksheet 2: Introduction to Creative Approaches (see page 105) could also be used at this stage, since it contains a simple breathing exercise and a story. Make sure that people do not feel more anxious through not knowing what they are doing or feeling that they have to conform to a set of expectations.

The exercises in this part can be discussed as a group and chosen to suit the context and preferences of participants. It is important that children and teenagers feel they have a choice, and they may be attracted to a particular title or theme of an exercise. Working with anxiety needs to be seen, as far as possible, as a partnership, with participants understanding that they can change or modify a technique, repeat it, or walk away if they wish.

Chapter 1

Nesting and Breathing

Exercise 1.1: Techniques to Explore 'Nesting' and Calm Breathing

Aims

- to encourage a feeling of calm and safety
- to understand active relaxation for reducing stress

Resources

- shawl or cotton blanket
- chair or mat
- crayons or coloured pens
- Worksheet 3: Cosy Places (see page 106)

Focus

Concentrate on places that feel comfortable to be in.

Introduction

Participants should be invited to sit in a comfy position on a chair or mat, and wrap a shawl or blanket around themselves if they wish. The facilitator addresses the group:

> OK. Let's get started. Let's think about a comfy nest where some anxiety can be kept at bay. That's a place where we feel comfortable and not under pressure from other people. When we are anxious, we are under enough pressure from ourselves!
>
> We are not going to discuss symptoms or triggers for your anxiety for the moment. I'm sure many people have asked you these questions already, so we are going to work with a different approach. Right now, we are going to concentrate on comfort.
>
> Think about where you feel most comfortable. For most people, it is somewhere at home, maybe their bedroom, for others, it is on the sofa in front of the television. Everyone has their most comfy place.
>
> Using Worksheet 3, read the question, look through the list of options, and answer either by ticking an option or giving your own answer using a few words or a simple drawing.

To Think About

Cosy places where we can relax may vary at different times, for instance according to our mood, the weather, and whether other people are around. For some of us, there may be a feeling that we are wasting time!

DOI: 10.4324/9781032256641-3

Exercise 1.2: Nesting 1

Aims

- to develop the power of the imagination to create pictures
- to encourage individual variations in images and colours

Resources

- shawl or cotton blanket
- chair or mat
- crayons or coloured pens
- Worksheet 4: The Nest (see page 107)

Focus

Think about the idea of a nest, somewhere warm and comfortable.

Introduction

When we are feeling low or unwell or worried, we often seek comfort through our clothes, food or bedding. These are all positive things, but it is not helpful if we drink too much or stuff ourselves with food. We might try relaxing in a warm bath instead!

To Do

Sit in a comfy position on a chair or mat, and wrap a shawl or blanket around yourself if you wish. Think about a nest as a place where you can relax and feel comfortable. What colours and textures does it have?

- Sit comfortably and breathe calmly.
- Think about the idea of a cosy nest.
- Use Worksheet 4 to draw or write about the qualities of your special nest.
- If you prefer to use your own ideas, use the reverse of the worksheet instead.
- Nests can be drawn or scribbled with lots of circles.

To Think About

Bedding these days has the feeling of providing more comfort, with duvets, flannelette sheets, and special colours, etc. – a big contrast to the austere and cold cotton and linen sheets of bygone times! If we feel comfortable outside, it may just help us to gain comfort inside.

Exercise 1.3: Nesting 2

Aims

- to continue feelings of calm and safety
- to understand using the imagination to reduce stress

Resources

- shawl or cotton blanket
- chair or mat
- crayons or coloured pens
- Worksheet 5: Breath Waves (see page 108)

Focus

Allow yourself to sit or lie in a relaxed way, and not hold on to tension.

Introduction

This calming exercise can be practised anywhere you can pause for a few moments: sitting, standing, or lying down. It can be done while standing in a queue at the supermarket or a bus stop, or while waiting for a class or an interview.

To Do

Sit in a comfy position on a chair or mat, and wrap a blanket or shawl around yourself if you wish. Remember your image of your nest and the place where you feel comfy. Use it now to help you feel calm.

- Take a deep breath, gently breathing in through your nose and out through your mouth. Repeat.
- Be aware of how your body feels when you are breathing.
- Just a few of these focused breaths can help to stop any escalation of anxiety (they can be practised anywhere).
- Using Worksheet 5, draw the waves of your breath – think about what colour they might be and what they look like.
- Now try drawing the waves at the same time as breathing, and try to synchronise the two movements.

To Think About

Our breathing is essential in everything we do, and we need to be aware of when we need lots of breath and do deep breathing, or when we may just need short breaths, like when we are having a conversation.

Remember: this exercise can be practised anywhere

Exercise 1.4: Breathing Basics

Aims

- to continue feelings of calm and safety
- to understand the variations in breathing

Resources

- shawl or cotton blanket
- chair or mat
- crayons or coloured pens
- completed copies of Worksheet 4: The Nest (see page 107) and Worksheet 5: Breath Waves (see page 108)

Focus

Concentrate on your breathing, and allow it to get slower and slower.

Introduction

Think about how we can picture something in our imaginations or see an image of it on a piece of paper in our hands. The better we are at picturing something in our minds, the more useful these exercises may be.

To Do

Sit in a comfy position on a chair or mat, and wrap a blanket or shawl around yourself if you wish. Make use of your nest picture, either in your imagination or the actual picture you created on Worksheet 4. Allow yourself to feel calmer by looking at the picture, and be aware of how you are breathing right now.

Think about the following breathing patterns, and try them out if you wish:

- Short, sharp breaths, almost like panting (using the upper chest), can be panic breathing.
- Deep breaths, rather like gulps or gasps (using the abdominal muscles), can be hyperventilation.
- Slow, deep breaths, like sighs (using the abdominal muscles), are often our breathing pattern when sleeping.
- Using Worksheet 5, draw your breath waves for the different types of breathing, using a different colour for each breath wave – notice if they have very different shapes.

To Think About

Our breathing has many variations and is often influenced by our mood. However, it is possible to change our breathing patterns and therefore change our mood. Most importantly, it is possible to reduce our anxiety levels.

Exercise 1.5: Starfish Relaxation 1

Aims

- to reduce feelings of tension
- to develop courage with body movements

Resources

- shawl or cotton blanket
- mat

Focus

Pay attention to your arms, and whether you are holding them in tension.

Introduction

If we hold our body in tension, it prevents our being able to breathe calmly. Experiment by holding your body very tensely and then trying to breathe – can you feel that there is no room inside for breath? We need to do focused breathing to relax, and then more breathing to expand.

To Do

Lie on your mat, and spread your blanket or shawl over you.

- Stretch your arms out as far as they will go, then let them go and relax them.
- Repeat the stretch and relax.
- Check that your breathing is relaxed.
- Repeat the stretch and relax one more time.
- Be aware of how your breathing changes when you stretch and relax.

To Think About

Take time to reflect on when and where your body feels uncomfortable and how easy it is to sit in a tense position without realising it. Our breathing is the key to changing our tension, and eventually, we will be able to 'let go' of tension

Exercise 1.6: Starfish Relaxation 2

Aims

- to continue to reduce feelings of tension
- to continue to develop courage with body movements

Resources

- shawl or cotton blanket
- mat

Focus

Focus on your legs, and whether you are holding them in tension.

Introduction

If we hold our body in tension, it prevents our being able to breathe calmly. We can experiment by holding our body very tense, and then discover that there is no room inside for breath! The more we can learn to relax physically, the more we can expand and develop our breathing. It is impossible to relax unless we change our breathing.

To Do

Lie on your mat, and spread your blanket or shawl over you.

- Stretch your legs out as far as they will go, then let them go and relax them.
- Repeat the stretch and relax.
- Check that your breathing is relaxed.
- Repeat the stretch and relax one more time.
- If you are feeling adventurous, try stretching both your legs and arms at once, and then letting go.
- Stay lying down in a relaxed position until you are ready to sit up.

To Think About

You may remember being told as a child, 'stand up straight', 'sit up and don't slouch', and some children used to be made to sit on stools at the table in order to keep their backs straight. All these instructions to stand up straight can cause tension if they are implemented in the wrong way – something for us all to think about!

Exercise 1.7: Starfish Relaxation 3

Aims

- to continue to develop and reduce feelings of tension
- to continue to develop courage with body movements

Resources

- shawl or cotton blanket
- mat

Focus

Focus on your legs and arms, and whether you are holding them in tension.

Introduction

In the previous exercises, we have discovered that if our bodies are tense, this prevents us from breathing calmly. In this exercise, we will try stretching our whole bodies in the starfish shape and see if it will allow us to breathe more comfortably. This is not just about our legs and arms, we also need to remember our faces, chests, and stomachs that can be held in tension.

To Do

Lie on your mat, spread your blanket or shawl over you, and check your breathing.

- Stretch your arms and legs out as far as they will go, like a starfish.
- Let your whole body go, and relax, breathing easily.
- Repeat this whole body stretch, then brace your chest muscles and relax.
- Pause for a moment and see if your breathing is staying relaxed.
- Try stretching your whole body one more time, and draw in your stomach muscles, then let everything go, and relax and breathe easily.

To Think About

You will notice as you repeat this exercise that your body is able to stretch more and able to relax more. However, be aware that often when we stretch, we restrict our breathing. We need to learn to breathe easily so that our breath can help relax our tense muscles and help them 'let go'.

Exercise 1.8: The Rhythm of Breathing

Aims

- to establish that breathing has its own rhythm and that anxiety can distort it
- to allow the experience of some control over breathing patterns

Resources

- shawl or cotton blanket
- mat

Focus

Concentrate on your heartbeat and the movement of your chest as you breathe.

Introduction

When we spend a little time being aware of how our rib cages work, we can feel how the muscles between our ribs expand and contract. This enables us to develop a greater breathing capacity and the ability to regulate the rhythm of our breaths.

To Do

Sit on your mat with a blanket or shawl wrapped around you, to feel warm and nurtured.

- Put your left hand on your rib cage and your right hand where your heart is.
- Be aware of the rhythm of your heartbeat.
- Breathe deeply, slowly in and out – notice how your rib cage expands and contracts.
- If your heartbeat is a little faster than usual, see if you can slow it down by deep breathing.
- Breathe in deeply and give a big sigh, and be aware both of your breathing and heartbeat.

To Think About

It is important that we become aware of the rhythms of our own heartbeats. We need to understand that we can change and regulate our heartbeats through our breathing.

Exercise 1.9: Experiencing Support

Aims

- to encourage participants to feel support from others
- to develop mutual trust between group members

Resources

- mat

Focus

Breathe calmly, and think about sharing work with a partner.

Introduction

When we feel anxious, we often isolate ourselves from other people and sometimes our anxiety can communicate itself to others. In this exercise, we will see if we can change the pattern of our anxiety in order to feel support from other people.

To Do

Sit on your mat, back-to-back with a partner. If you feel comfortable doing so, lean against your partner. Go through this following sequence as you sit on your mats together:

- As you breathe, be aware of the person sitting behind you.
- See if you can synchronise your breathing so you both breathe out at the same time.
- Take it in turns to change your breathing pattern so one of you follows the other.
- Finish with some very deep breathing in order to relax.
- Turn around and face your partner, and discuss how it felt to have synchronised breathing.

To Think About

Before babies are born, they are very aware of the breathing of their mothers, which influences their own breathing patterns. Think about how we can be aware of someone else's breathing patterns and the fact we can synchronise them together.

Exercise 1.10: Imagining Kindness

Aims

- to encourage the imagination to remember someone who has been kind
- to remember the feelings associated with that kind person

Resources

- shawl or cotton blanket
- mat

Focus

Try and recall someone who has been kind to you and what they said or did.

Introduction

It is important for us to recall any times in our lives when people have been kind to us. It may have been a friend or someone in a shop, or maybe a particular teacher. But with recall, individuals can recognise the feelings associated with other people's kindness.

To Do

Sit on your mat, wrapped in your blanket or shawl if you wish, again sitting back-to-back with a partner if you feel comfortable doing so, breathing slowly in and out, and if sitting in pairs, being aware of your partner's breathing rhythms.

- Recall somebody in your life, at any age, who was kind to you.
- Remember the feeling when you experienced somebody else's kindness, and what they said or did.
- Think about whether this kindness was expected or a pleasant surprise.
- Allow that feeling to stay with you, and continue the steady breathing.
- Turn around and face your partner, and share the act of kindness you have remembered if you wish.

To Think About

Whatever our experiences of other people's criticisms or unpleasantness, when people are kind to us, it makes a big difference to how we experience the world. It can change the feeling of 'everyone is against me' to 'maybe some people are against me, but others support me'. That is a very big step!

CBT Exercises

1. Sit upright in your chair, scrunch up your body and face as tight as you can, and hold your breath for the count of three. Then let all your muscles go, and blow out. Wait for 10 seconds. Repeat the scrunch and blow. Repeat one more time, and notice how your body has changed how it feels.
2. Walk around the room, then sit again, upright in your chair. Breathe in through your nose, then blow your breath out slowly through your mouth. Repeat, and hold your breath for a count of three before blowing out again. Repeat one more time, then notice whether your body is less tense and you feel less stressed.

Working Online

All these exercises can be done online, and indeed some people may feel safer online than doing the exercises in person. However, in this context I recommend doing all the exercises seated in a chair, and not lying on the floor. Lying on the floor can make people feel very vulnerable.

Summary

Chapter 1 is about harnessing our breathing to help reduce anxiety. We need to be aware of how we set up a situation so that we do not increase anxiety. Sitting and talking is not necessarily helpful for young people – they often need to move and take action. The practices described in this chapter are supported by Polyvagal Theory, which emphasises feeling safe and the body being the main focus for change.

Questions and Reflections for Discussion

1. What part does anxiety play in your own life? What do you find works for you?
2. Reports suggest that child and teenage anxiety has increased recently – why do you think this is?
3. What are your own ideas to reduce the incidence of anxiety for everyone?

Chapter 2

Solutions for Sleep

Anxiety and insomnia are intertwined: people who are anxious have difficulty sleeping, and with lack of sleep, people become more anxious as their performance level gets worse, they are increasingly irritable and anti-social, and have decreasing self-confidence.

There is a huge range of theories regarding what causes people to have difficulty sleeping, and it seems that for a large number of people there is an actual event or concern that stops them sleeping. When it is removed, people are usually able to sleep again. According to Schmidt and Van der Linden (2011), there is another group for whom the difficulty is their apprehension at giving up control of themselves and their lives when they fall asleep. Fear of giving up control seems to be apparent in many children and teenagers, who appear to develop hypervigilance when their sleeplessness becomes chronic. A range of sensory stimuli can trigger hypervigilance, including:

- feeling trapped
- struggles with breathing
- sudden noises
- uncertainty
- arguments
- anxiety about nightmares
- overstimulation
- fear of dying

Hypervigilance can be about self-preservation or about looking after and protecting other people. It is often associated with feelings of injustice or victimisation (Savva 2016).

Some young people may have memories of being locked in a cupboard, being made to lie in a medical scanner, or being zipped into an infant gas mask. There can be many examples of not being able to escape or even move, and these memories may have been buried for a very long time.

Creative Arts Exercises

In Chapter 2, Exercises 2.1–2.5 are intended to help children and young people *prepare* for better sleep, Exercises 2.6–2.10 should give them the tools they need to help them *fall asleep* once they are in bed.

Many people have difficulty with sleep when they feel anxious. They may fall asleep briefly, and wake up feeling fearful. They may fall asleep for a longer time, and wake suddenly feeling very scared, or they may have trouble falling asleep at all.

People who are anxious often don't get enough sleep, and the lack of sleep adds to existing feelings of inadequacy and lack of confidence. Negative thoughts and worries will go round and round in their heads and produce such tension that their heartbeat can start to race and they may feel hot and cold or they may get stomach pains. One way to begin to address this is to develop a bedtime routine that is simple to implement and which the person feels they have control over.

Exercises 2.1–2.5 in this chapter are designed to counter some of the intrusive thoughts that prevent people sleeping by starting to replace anxious thoughts and situations with recollections of soothing voices, chants, rhythms, and singing. In this way, people will be able to begin to decrease the possibility of negative experiences intruding on their sleep.

Exercises 2.6–2.10 are directly related to using soothing and relaxing strategies to prepare to go to sleep at night.

DOI: 10.4324/9781032256641-4

Exercise 2.1: Preliminary Mindfulness 1

Aims

- to help people prepare to be more relaxed at bedtime
- to introduce mindfulness as a way of addressing anxiety

Resources

- shawl or cotton blanket
- mat

Focus

Keep your breathing calm, and think about whether anywhere in your body feels tense.

Introduction

Many people with anxiety find that they simply cannot get themselves into a comfortable physical position, and that this really prevents them from sleeping. They may briefly fall asleep, but can wake up again and again, feeling uncomfortable.

To Do

Lie on your mat in a comfortable position – this might be curled up, on your side, or on your back. Now do some regular deep breathing, using some of the techniques you have learned in earlier exercises.

- Be aware of the sounds and sensations of your breathing.
- Allow yourself to focus on the rise and fall of your chest as you breathe.
- Be aware of the texture of your clothes and how they touch and feel against your skin.
- Allow your breathing to get deeper and deeper.
- Make sure that you are keeping your body very relaxed.

To Think About

Be aware of those moments as you are lying quietly when you get tense again. Is it a habit, or has an anxious thought popped into your mind? Try to relax again and reduce any tensions by focusing on the rhythm of your breathing.

Exercise 2.2: Preliminary Mindfulness 2

Aims

- to continue to help people prepare to be more relaxed at bedtime
- to continue to introduce mindfulness as a way of addressing anxiety

Resources

- shawl or cotton blanket
- mat

Focus

Close your eyes, and try to relax and focus on the rhythm of your breathing.

Introduction

It is easy for people to say to us, 'Just relax and go to sleep!', but it is not that simple. We may have patterns established from early childhood when we were scared of the dark, or we may have worries or fears that we can't let go of once we are in bed. By thinking of a calm and safe place, we can begin to relax and replace the worries.

To Do

Sit on your mat, wrapped in your blanket or shawl if you wish, concentrate on your breathing, and try to focus on images of your safe 'nest' in your head.

*   Think about your ideas for your 'nest'.
*   Remember what qualities it had – its texture, its colour, the sounds.
*   Try to picture the nest as a whole in your imagination.
*   Check that your breathing is still calm.
*   Try and hold the picture of your nest in your mind for several minutes and continue to feel calm.

To Think About

We need to be able to recall calming pictures that we may have stored away and maybe even forgotten about. Thinking about and bringing to mind a calm image can help us relax. It could be our safe and comfortable 'nest', or a seaside or landscape, or a house, or even a person we feel safe around that will help us to maintain a state of relaxation with calm breathing.

Exercise 2.3: Calming Voices 1

Aims

*   to raise awareness of the soothing qualities in people's voices
*   to raise awareness that we could change our own voices

Resources

*   shawl or cotton blanket
*   mat

Focus

Think about relaxing your body and calming your breathing.

Introduction

We can become anxious as children when we are shouted at or ridiculed. The power of other people's voices can stay with us as we become teenagers, and the original source of the shouting can be forgotten. We need to be aware of voices and their influences on our levels of anxiety.

To Do

Sit on your mat, wrapped in your blanket or shawl if you wish.

*   Sit calmly, and check your breathing.
*   Think about a voice you remember from your life that had a very soothing quality – it can be anyone, whether you know them or not.
*   Did you hear this voice when you were much younger, or is it a voice belonging to someone you hear or know now?
*   Try to hear the voice in your head now.
*   Allow yourself to hear this voice saying something kind to you.
*   Try to store the memory of this voice in your mind to be aware of when you get anxious.

To Think About

Very often, we can recognise people by their voices even if we can't see them. Everybody is influenced by people's voices, even before they are born. Did you know that the mother's womb acts like an amplifier, so that the baby hears the mother's voice much louder than in ordinary life?

Exercise 2.4: Calming Voices 2

Aims

- to recall childhood songs or chants that are calming
- to be aware of the rhythmic nature of songs and chants which have a calming effect

Resources

- shawl or cotton blanket
- mat

Focus

Think of positive, playful memories in your childhood. Maybe someone sang to you or there were percussion rhythms or chants.

Introduction

Teenagers may believe that nursery songs and chants are too childish , to think about now. However, for many children and young people, they will have had a calming influence. It is helpful if we can recall songs and even rhythmic games in our heads.

To Do

Sit quietly on your mat, wrapped in your blanket or shawl if you wish, and breathe calmly, breathing in through your nose and out through your mouth. If you are comfortable with this exercise, breathe in to a slow count of five, hold your breath for five, then slowly breathe out for five.

- Think about when you were younger and other people sang nursery rhymes or clapping games (make sure these are positive memories, and not nasty ones).
- Maybe you sang the songs with teachers, or with your grandparents or parents, or with other children in the playground.
- Think about the words that were repeated and the rhythm that was constant.
- Allow yourself to feel calm while you are remembering a song.
- Keep that rhythm and song in your head to think about when you get anxious.

To Think About

When we are feeling anxious, we often rock back and forwards, or even make repetitive movements with our hands or fingers without being aware we are doing it. This is something from very early in life – rocking and movements can be soothing. We can continue to use them whenever we feel anxious. Most of us got used to a rocking movement when we were rocked in the womb.

Exercise 2.5: Bedtime Stories I

Aims

- to encourage people to relax and allow themselves to hear a story
- to develop the security of storytelling as a positive influence

Resources

- shawl or cotton blanket
- mat
- Story Sheet 1: The Sewing of the Stars (see page 134)

Focus

Remember your calm breathing, and think about telling stories.

Introduction

It is important to convey that storytelling is for everyone, regardless of age and background. There is a part of our brain that gets stimulated when we hear stories. Often, we internalise negative stories about ourselves and imagine they have come from other people. Gradually, we may use stories to let go of negativity and encourage more positive feelings.

To Do

Sit or lie down in a comfortable position on your mat, and cover yourself with your blanket or shawl if you wish. The facilitator reads out the story of 'The Sewing of the Stars' from Story Sheet 1.

- Allow yourself to remember pleasant times of storytelling when you were younger.
- Listen to the story, and allow the images to float through your mind.
- If it is a story that is unusual, make a note in your mind of how it differs from other stories.
- If you don't remember all of the story, it doesn't matter, as you can have a copy of it.
- Hold onto any parts of the story that you find interesting.

To Think About

This story is about ancient China, when every village had a wise person. Nowadays, we often don't think about there being a wise person who can give advice or be kind to us. Do you have a wise person in your life? Who would you like it to be if you had the choice?

Exercise 2.6: Preparation for Sleep 1

Special Note

These techniques are to be applied at home, but their elements can be practised in the school or therapy room. It can also be helpful for parents to understand these routines and be given worksheets and story sheets to assist with the application.

Aims

- to encourage children and young people to begin to prepare to go to bed at least an hour in advance
- to highlight different factors that make sleeping difficult

Resources

None needed.

Focus

Think about the time you spend before going to bed and whether the things you do could be more restful.

Introduction

It is important that we have a routine surrounding bedtime. Unfortunately, we often sabotage our sleep by watching screens late in the evening and forget that a calming routine will enable us to sleep better.

To Do

Try the following routine and see if it makes a difference to your sleep pattern:

- Give yourself a definite time for going to bed.
- Switch off all of your screens at least one hour beforehand.
- Choose a warm drink, such as hot chocolate or herbal tea, that you find soothing.
- Take time to have a bath if you want, and to brush your teeth, but be aware of your calm breathing while you are doing so.
- Change into your nightclothes, get into bed, and try to use the relaxation and calm breathing exercises you have learned until you fall asleep.

To Think About

This is a very simple routine for us to follow, and will help reduce our anxiety by taking control of our breathing. However, it may need to be repeated over a period of time in order to drop off to sleep. Don't worry if it doesn't work right away – changes to routines take time to work.

Exercise 2.7: Preparation for Sleep 2

Special Note

These techniques are to be applied at home, but their elements can be practised in the school or therapy room. It can also be helpful for parents to understand these routines and be given worksheets and story sheets to assist with the application.

Aims

- to explore relaxation through a calming bath or shower
- to be aware of the senses that help us feel soothed

Resources

- scented candles (LED tea lights can be used if safety is an issue)
- scented bath oils or shower gels

Focus

Keeping a calm atmosphere for the bedtime routine.

Introduction

If we soak in a hot bath or take a warm shower, we can feel more relaxed. By reducing light, we can create a more restful atmosphere. Scented candles can also help.

To Do

Create an atmosphere of calm as you plan your bedtime routine. Switch off all screens, and focus on your bath.

- Put towels and pyjamas on a warm radiator.
- If possible, use scented candles to create a calm atmosphere.
- Soak in warm water and take time to wash, or have a warm shower – this will help the whole of your body to relax.
- Be careful not to let the water get cold, so you can leave the warm water and wrap yourself in a warm towel.
- Pat yourself dry, and put on warm pyjamas.

To Think About

Warm water can be very relaxing, whether in a bath or a shower. We can also have warm water in a hot water bottle for when we sleep. A hot drink at bedtime can also be soothing, providing it is caffeine-free!

Exercise 2.8: Preparation for Sleep 3

Special Note

These techniques are to be applied at home, but their elements can be practised in the school or therapy room. It can also be helpful for parents to understand these routines and be given worksheets and story sheets to assist with the application.

Aims

- to learn how to maintain breathing levels in order to encourage sleep
- to re-focus on positive images that don't intrude on sleep patterns

Resources

None needed.

Focus

To release the tension that permits negative images to intrude and to focus on positive ones instead.

Introduction

Many of us are frightened to fall asleep because we experience negative images or bad dreams and can wake up feeling frightened. These exercises can help us to control what we allow ourselves to visualise, whether awake or asleep.

To Do

Try to remember all the cosy and comfy things that can be comforting at bedtime.

- Think about wearing fleecy pyjamas.
- Try to decide which position is most comfortable for you – for example, do you prefer to lie on your side or on your back?
- Do you have a cuddly toy that you like to take to bed, or maybe a soft blanket?
- Whatever it is, hug it close to you and use its texture to stroke your cheek.
- Breathe in through your nose and out through your mouth – try and breathe slower and slower until you fall asleep.

To Think About

When we are kept awake at night, we need to be aware of any images that are preventing us from sleeping. These could be events from the daytime or thoughts of scary things that might happen, or random thoughts about success or failure, popularity or unpopularity. Try to focus on what these waking periods are really about.

Exercise 2.9: Bedtime Stories 2

Aims

- to encourage memories of pleasurable stories for staying calm
- to focus on positive stories that don't intrude on the sleep pattern

Resources

None needed.

Focus

Breathe deeply while thinking about a positive story or event from the past.

Introduction

Sometimes, we can be frightened to fall asleep because we remember negative stories or bad experiences that keep us awake. This exercise can help us to control the stories we choose to focus on.

To Do

Try to remember all of the things that can be comforting while you are in bed.

*   Remember to wear comfortable nightclothes.
*   Decide which position is most comfortable – for example, on your side or on your back.
*   Try to recall any stories you were told or read as a child that you really enjoyed.
*   Focus on one of these stories now, and try to remember what you enjoyed about it.
*   As you recall the story, smile at the memory and continue your relaxed breathing.

To Think About

If you can't go to sleep at night, try to be aware of the thoughts and stories that are keeping you awake. Are they from the media or news? Or are you worrying about scary things that might happen? Try to let go of these thoughts and replace them with stories that are more enjoyable.

Exercise 2.10: Bedtime Stories 3

Aims

*   to help people to relax and allow themselves to remember a story
*   to encourage the security of storytelling as a positive influence

Resources

*   Story Sheet 1: The Sewing of the Stars (see page 134)

Focus

Recall, if you can, what you can remember of the story 'The Sewing of the Stars'.

Introduction

It is important to remember that storytelling is for everyone, regardless of age and background. There is a part of our brain that becomes engaged when we hear stories, and repeating stories always makes us think of new issues.

To Do

When you are in your home, lie comfortably in your bed in cosy pyjamas and with the covers pulled up.

*   Breathe in through your nose, and blow gently out through your mouth.
*   Try to recall the story about 'The Sewing of the Stars'.
*   Picture the image of the vast, dark sky that had stars sewn into it.
*   If you have heard the story before, what do you remember now?
*   What was the most important thing for you in this story?

Alternatively, during the session, imagine the situation at home, relax on cushions with a blanket or shawl, and go through the same process of recalling the story.

To Think About

Continue to recall favourite stories from when you were young. Did you read them for yourself, or did someone read to you? You could try to listen to a story or audiobook as you go to sleep.

CBT Exercises

- Keep a sleep diary, and write down your patterns of being awake and asleep and whether there is anything specific keeping you from sleeping.
- Sit quietly and think of the negative thoughts that keep you awake. Try to replace them with positive thoughts that might allow you to sleep.

Working Online

All the breathing and relaxation exercises can be worked with online. Having a calm discussion with children or teenagers online about preparation for bedtime can help to establish new routines.

Summary

This chapter addressed the issue of insomnia, and new routines that can help to change tension and prepare for sleep. It discussed hypervigilance and issues of control. The calming exercises and CBT techniques aim to interrupt fixed patterns of tension.

Questions and Reflections for Discussion

1. Reflect on your own hypervigilance or watchfulness.
2. What are the things that keep you awake at night?
3. Have you slept in fits and starts with a small child?
4. As a child yourself, did you have bad dreams?
5. What were your favourite stories and rhymes as a child?

Sleep, Relaxation, and Light

This chapter continues the theme of sleep, and describes further relaxation exercises that can be used for general relaxation or release of sleep-related tension. There are some useful ideas in the book *Self-regulation Skills in Young Children* (Asquith 2020). In particular, Sue Asquith discusses white noise and how some children sleep better with certain types of noise in the background. Please see Appendix 2 for more information about white noise.

We also need to be aware of how lighting can affect both anxiety and sleeplessness. Many young people become very anxious if there is no light at all. Bedside lamps that can be dimmed gently in stages by touching the base can be very helpful. They can easily be switched between levels for reading and for trying to relax, and the lowest light level can be used for falling asleep without having bright lights in a bedroom.

Exercise 3.1: Whole-body Relaxation

Aims

- to be aware of whole-body relaxation to promote sleep
- to take control of muscle tension and relaxation to get rid of anxiety

Resources

None needed.

Focus

Be aware of your whole body and how some parts can become tense.

Introduction

Many people find they have only relaxed parts of their body, leaving other parts in tension. This exercise describes a whole-body approach where every part of the body from the toes to the head is in a state of relaxation – or tries to be!

To Do

At home, lie comfortably in your bed with the light turned low, and close your eyes if possible.

- Starting with your toes and feet, work your way up your body doing the following exercises for your feet, legs, buttocks, stomach, chest, hands, arms, shoulders, neck, and face.
- Clench and relax the muscles of each body part.
- With each muscle tensing and release, just focus on one particular body part.
- When you have tensed and relaxed the whole of your body from your feet to your forehead, go back and check that nothing else has tensed up meanwhile.

Alternatively, you can follow the same instructions during a session, with a mat, cushions, and a blanket or shawl.

DOI: 10.4324/9781032256641-5

To Think About

After this whole-body relaxation, you may find it easier to fall asleep, to drift off, especially if it is accompanied by slow, deep breathing. Even if you are not actually asleep, you can try to keep in a state of total relaxation without tensing

Exercise 3.2: Whole-body Awareness

Aims

- to be aware of the whole body and which parts tense up
- to be alert when muscles and limbs become tense

Resources

None needed.

Focus

Whole-body awareness for tension and relaxation.

Introduction

We can be surprised when we discover parts of our bodies can return to tension after a relaxation exercise. Old habits die hard, as the saying goes, and we have to re-learn our physical patterns and easy breathing.

To Do

At home, lie comfortably in your bed.

- Breathe deeply in through your nose and out through your mouth, very slowly, allowing it to go deeper and deeper.
- Do a body check of which muscles have tensed up – it is often the shoulders.
- In your mind, send a message to your shoulders that they are not carrying any burdens.
- Allow your shoulders to relax, and check any other parts of your body.
- Continue the deep breathing.

Alternatively, you can follow the same instructions during a session, using a mat, cushions, and a blanket or shawl.

To Think About

It is not easy to maintain a state of relaxation, but the deeper we sleep, the more refreshed we will be in the daytime. Doctors of all persuasions are recommending we get eight hours of sleep – preferably some of it before midnight!

Exercise 3.3: Relaxing in Our Surroundings

Aims

- understanding the elements in our environment that stop us from sleeping
- learning to make connections between what we can control and what feels overwhelming

Resources

None needed.

Focus

Reflect on your sleeping environment and whether it helps you sleep or makes you alert.

Introduction

The atmosphere of our bedroom makes an impact on our ability to sleep well – it is not just a question of sleeping, but sleeping deeply for enough hours. Maybe the decorations are too stimulating or the lighting too harsh. It is important to give some consideration to what's around you when you try to sleep.

To Do

At home, concentrate on your surroundings in your bedroom.

- Take time to sit up in your bed and look around the room to see if anything is overstimulating.
- Maybe you could change some of the colours to be more calming.
- Maybe you need to look at the lighting to see if it is too harsh (for example, strip lighting).
- Do you have favourite music you listen to that is relaxing?
- Keep a notebook and pen by your bed to note down any changes you would like to make.

Alternatively, imagine the situation in your bedroom at home, and make some notes of things you might change.

To Think About

Sometimes, we are just given a room without any say in how it looks – maybe a room that has belonged to a sibling, with their preferred colours and lighting. Think of ways to make it yours, and it may give you a calmer atmosphere.

Exercise 3.4: Sleeping with Light

Aims

- to understand how our circadian rhythm (our biological 24-hour clock) is affected by light (see Appendix 2)
- to be aware of our own capacity to control the light and dark sequences

Resources

None needed.

Focus

Relax and focus on the surroundings where you sleep.

Introduction

The power of light is very important to understanding our sleep patterns. Some people are unable to sleep when the room is totally blacked out. Others struggle when there is too much light. Having screens on at bedtime exposes us to artificial light that sends mixed messages to our brains.

To Do

Sit up in bed, feeling comfortable.

- Just concentrate on the amount of light in your room.
- Is it coming from inside the room, or outside?
- Do you feel more comfortable with the curtains open, or closed?
- Do you like your bedroom door open, or shut?
- Is it important to know the landing light is on?

To Think About

Bear in mind that reading a book or looking at pictures in a book is a very calming activity. It is quite the opposite of looking at screens. Think about having two sorts of bedside lamp: one that is dim and soothing, and one that is bright so you can read if you wish. (You can buy lamps that have multiple light levels that change if you touch them.)

Exercise 3.5: Lamps and Lights

Aims

- to increase awareness of how light affects our mood
- to encourage decision-making about appropriate light in our own environment

Resources

- shawl or cotton blanket
- mat or chair and table
- crayons or coloured pens
- Worksheet 6: Lamps and Lights (see page 109)

Focus

Concentrate on your close and wider environment, and be aware that different types of lighting influence how you are feeling.

Introduction

It is very important that we develop an awareness of our surroundings, particularly in relation to light and dark. It is also important to realise we have the power to change it if we want.

To Do

Sit comfortably at a table or on your mat, wrapped in your blanket or shawl if you wish, with colouring materials and Worksheet 6.

- Close your eyes and maintain an even breathing rhythm.
- Picture as many different types of light as you can think of: candles, street lighting, strip lights, desk lamps, etc.
- Look at the range of lights on the worksheet.
- Think about which lights you like more than others, and colour them in.
- Use the worksheet to make decisions about how you would like to change the lighting in your environment.

To Think About

Light and lack of it has been an important theme throughout history. It has featured in many stories, and is essential to many religions. For social anxiety, it is important to be aware of how lighting affects our lives.

Exercise 3.6: Festivals of Light

Aims

- to introduce festivals of light that occur in several cultures
- to increase understanding of the meanings behind the festivals

Resources

- shawl or cotton blanket
- mat or chair and table
- crayons or coloured pens
- Worksheet 7: Festivals of Light – Diwali (see page 110)

Focus

Try to concentrate on the difference between the light in summer and in winter.

Introduction

Many cultures have festivals of light. In ancient times in the UK, the festival of light, Samhain, marked the transition at the end of October and beginning of November, and the Hindu festival of Diwali also occurs in the autumn. The celebration of Guy Fawkes' Night on 5 November was superimposed on the existing festival of light during which bonfires were lit, particularly around coastal regions.

To Do

Think about how cultures use dance and drama and rituals to celebrate festivals of light.

- While thinking about light, remember that fear of the dark is a cultural fear, not just an individual one.
- Reflect on how increasing light can actually decrease your fear of the dark.
- Looking at Worksheet 7, which of the festivals of light do you find interesting?
- Spent some time colouring the decorations on the worksheet, remembering that all festivals of light use very bright colours as well as lanterns and lamps.
- Create a border of lamps around the worksheet with your favourite types of lamps.

To Think About

It can help us reduce our anxiety if we remember that fear of the dark is very common, both for individuals and for groups. Having a mild light in your bedroom, your bedroom door open to see the light on the landing, or a torch by your bedside will help you to keep calmer about darkness.

Exercise 3.7: The Lighthouse I

Aims

- to introduce the metaphor of the lighthouse as a means of light alleviating danger
- to introduce the idea of lighthouses assisting us to understand danger

Resources

- shawl or cotton blanket
- mat
- crayons or coloured pens
- Worksheet 8: The Lighthouse (see page 111)

Focus

Sit in a relaxed way, and think about the image of the lighthouse shining in the dark.

Introduction

The image of the lighthouse, where the blinking light warns ships that surrounding rocks are very dangerous, is an important metaphor to help us reduce our anxiety. For many people, the imagined danger is being washed up on the rocks of life and being overpowered by turbulent water.

To Do

As you sit comfortably, be aware of the light and dark images in the lighthouse – there is an outline of a lighthouse on Worksheet 8.

- Make sure your breathing is calm and even.
- Think about the colours of a lighthouse – it has solid walls and tiny windows.

- What is the base of the lighthouse? It has to have some kind of path leading to it in order for lighthouse keepers to have access.
- Colour in the worksheet, indicating the hazardous rocks and water, and perhaps showing ships sailing past.
- Imagine what it would be like to be steering a ship and making sure that the rocks were avoided.

To Think About

The idea of people being in danger because of rocks and stormy weather can reflect very much how we feel. We often talk about shifting sands or being swamped. There are many land and weather metaphors to describe our feelings.

Exercise 3.8: The Lighthouse 2

Aims

- to introduce the lighthouse keeper as a calm and patient role
- to encourage identification with a lighthouse keeper

Resources

- shawl or cotton blanket
- mat

Focus

Think about what you would need if you were going to live in a lighthouse for three months.

Introduction

Although most lighthouses are now controlled automatically, there are still some that need a lighthouse keeper to operate the lights manually. Usually, lighthouse keepers will go to a lighthouse for three months with enough provisions to last that time. The weather may be too stormy to catch any fish!

To Do

Sit comfortably, and think about what it would be like to live in a lighthouse.

- If you were the lighthouse keeper, what would you need to survive for three months?
- Think about the food you would need.
- What would you do with your time, from switching the lights off in the morning to switching them on when it got dark in the evening?
- Would it be hard if there was no Wi-Fi?
- Would you want to draw or colour or perhaps make a model with some clay? Think of the things you would have time to do that you couldn't do with your day now.

To Think About

When we are anxious, is may be easier for some to be with other people, and for others to be on their own. Would living in a lighthouse be very difficult for you because of being on your own for a few months? Does this prospect cause you more anxiety, or less?

Exercise 3.9: Lighthouse Bedtime Story

Aims

- to connect the lighthouse image to a story that describes the life of a lighthouse keeper
- to understand the story as having unusual elements

Resources

- shawl or cotton blanket
- mat
- crayons or coloured pens
- Story Sheets 2 and 3: The Lighthouse Keeper, Parts 1 and 2 (see pages 135 and 136) and Worksheet 8: The Lighthouse (see page 111)

Focus

Concentrate on the image of the lighthouse on Worksheet 8 and the character in the story called Jem, who had an interesting experience while he was working.

Introduction

The lighthouse story is one of many folk tales that surround the lives of lighthouse keepers and lighthouses. The relationships of lighthouse keepers with the sea can become like fairy stories. They are often associated with mermaids and silkies. They challenge people's imagination to think outside the box.

To Do

The facilitator reads the story while you follow it on Story Sheets 2 and 3, sitting calmly.

- Think about the fact that Jem became ill with a fever.
- Did that change his perception of what was going on?
- Make your own decision about what you think happened.
- Colour the picture on Worksheet 8.
- Think about other folk tales where something unusual happens.

To Think About

This story allows us to imagine different things that could happen in different situations. The story of Jem gives us a very positive image of the silkie as the helper. It also is important in the way it shows how a relationship developed between Jem and the silkie – one of mutual care and concern.

Exercise 3.10: The Buried Moon Story

Aims

- to illustrate cultural awareness of light and dark
- to introduce the impact of the phases of the moon (light and dark)

Resources

- shawl or cotton blanket
- mat
- crayons or coloured pens
- Story Sheet 4: The Buried Moon (see page 137)

Focus

Relax and breathe calmly, and think about images of the moon.

Introduction

The story of the buried moon is a very powerful tale that shows how communities can empower themselves when they feel there is a human need or when they are in danger.

To Do

Sit comfortably, and prepare to listen to 'The Buried Moon'.

- Follow the story as it is being read.
- Decide which part of the story impresses you most.
- The role of the wise woman in this story is very important – what sort of person do you think she would be?
- When the story is finished, think of an illustration for this story that you think is appropriate, then draw it on the back of the story sheet.
- Think about the bog people and their power to grab hold of people, and how the people were able to avoid them.

To Think About

Pay attention to the contrast in the story between the light of the moon in the sky and the darkness of the bog people in the swamp, and how the village people rely on the illumination of the moon to guide them through their daily routine. Maybe discover more moon stories by researching on the internet.

Notes

- There is some flexibility in how these exercises are applied. For example, there may be some anxiety about giving instructions for people to work in their own beds and bedrooms.
- Almost all of Chapter 3 can be adapted to a class or group.
- Don't be surprised if some people actually fall asleep!
- There can still be hot chocolate as a nurturing drink!
- Participants may like to have a notebook where they can write down exercises to try at home.
- The only exercise that may prove tricky in the class is the bath or shower!
- Be aware that some people may not be able to read, but they can have copies of the stories and follow them while they are being read.

CBT Exercises

1. Using paper and coloured pencils, draw very slow and gentle patterns, and be aware of your breathing slowing down while you draw. End by giving a big sigh. How would you draw that?
2. Write down: one thing to remember to help you sleep; two things that sound restful; three things that feel restful.

Working Online

All of these exercises can be adapted when working online. Bed and shower techniques for sleeping and relaxation can be tested online if participants wish to try them out while sitting in a comfy chair, in which case the shower or bath routine will have to be imagined.

Summary

Chapter 3 focused on sleep itself: how to prepare for sleep, and how to fall asleep. It considered different sensory elements that can induce sleep, especially clothing, warm baths, and so on. Lighthouse stories and metaphors allow us to develop our imagination to break patterns of stress.

Questions and Reflections for Discussion

1. Are you a light or a deep sleeper?
2. How did you sleep as a child?
3. Can you remember any scary things that prevented you sleeping?
4. What would you do if a child you were teaching kept falling asleep in class?
5. How would you introduce the idea of 'nesting' to teenagers?

Summary of Part I

In this part, the focus has been mainly on anxiety that causes sleeplessness, and ways to change patterns of anxiety through breathing, mindfulness, changes in our environment, and adjustments to lighting. There are several stories that can help to change fixed patterns of thinking, as well as descriptions of worksheets with exercises for change. Throughout, there has been an emphasis on children's and teenagers' freedom of choice, and that no one should be forced to do an exercise. The questions and reflections at the end of each chapter may help teachers, therapists, and parents gain a greater understanding of their own anxiety and insomnia.

Remember

It is very important that we pay enough attention to our own self-care:

- Are we getting enough sleep?
- Is anxiety affecting our parenting, teaching, or therapeutic work?

Part II

Perception, Feelings, and Safety

Introduction

There are three chapters in Part II of this book: 'How Do I See My Anxiety?', 'Faces and Feelings', and 'Where Is My Safe Place?'

In Chapter 4, we will develop ideas for feeling secure and comfortable through learning to control our breathing. Chapter 5 will cover ideas for improving our sleeping patterns, and Chapter 6 will describe nurturing techniques to allow people to self-soothe.

Part II is about how we see our anxiety and being able to give it a shape or form through drawing or modelling, as well as in our imagination. There are also techniques for growing awareness of places where we can feel safe, and not anxious. The titles of the three chapters in this part reflect these topics.

Deb Dana, who practises Polyvagal Theory, suggests we need to go back to body basics and learn the most basic breathing techniques. She says:

> Breath is an autonomic action that can be intentionally manipulated and is a direct route to influencing the autonomic state. When your clients use these exercises between sessions, they are practicing regulation. When you join your clients in following their breath it becomes a co-regulating activity.
>
> (Dana 2021, p.131)

It is hoped that having developed security by working through Part I, children and young people may now be able to consider their anxiety in more detail with specific content. It is also important to be able to develop a timeline, as not all anxiety starts in childhood. There may be a specific event or traumatic episode that resulted in enduring anxiety. It is not always possible to recall things that happened in our early childhood, though we may have been told about any early trauma. Domestic violence, different types of abuse and multiple changes of homes, schools, and carers can all feed anxiety in children and become embedded by the time they reach their teens.

Many young people try to hide their anxiety by 'cover-up' dressing and hairstyles. Anxious children may talk about being unwell, manifested through various symptoms such as headaches or tummy pains. They may also hide behind a family role, such as 'Jane's always been shy, just like her mother.'

Anxious teenagers are often labelled by teachers or parents, and sometimes these labels stick. Many children and teenagers feel humiliated by a label or nickname, especially when it is not of their own choosing:

> She's just shy – rather attractive in a girl, don't you think?
> Tom always sits at the back of the class, he seems more comfortable there.

This labelling is actually lazy, as it prevents adults from really thinking about what needs to be addressed. For some teachers, it may be a blessed relief that at least someone in the class is quiet!

As one young person said, 'You can't get hold of it, it's slippery, and just when you think you've got it, it's gone again and slips back somewhere else.'

Pause for a moment and think back to your own childhood or teens. Can you remember labels or nicknames you were given? Did they stick? How did you feel about it? Maybe write your answers in your journal.

In Part II, we will explore in greater detail how faces can excite fear and how we often categorise facial expressions (Chapter 4, 'How Do I See My Anxiety?'). Following the nurturing theme of the whole book, we will devote time and space to the theme of kind faces and whether it is possible to change our own facial expressions to show kindness and concern (Chapter 5, 'Faces and Feelings').

We will then explore the theme of places that feel safe and unsafe (Chapter 6, 'Where Is My Safe Place?'). We all have places that do not feel comfortable or where, as a young child, we felt scared.

DOI: 10.4324/9781032256641-6

Learning Outcomes for Part II

- understanding how we perceive our anxiety – how does it look?
- encouraging the expression of feelings about kindness
- exploring the places where we feel safe – both in reality and in our imagination

---

Example

One 11-year-old who attended play sessions for anxiety gave a wide berth to the rest area with its cushions and blankets. It later emerged that one of her cousins (who turned out to be a half-sibling) had said he would kill her, and had put an eiderdown over her face and then laid on top of her, trying to suffocate her. She eventually fought him off, but came up spluttering and gasping for air. The fact that neither set of parents believed her made it doubly worse.

Chapter 4

How Do I See My Anxiety?

Exercise 4.1: My Anxious Hand 1

Aims

- to introduce the connection between body states and anxiety
- to encourage people to be more precise regarding the actual location of their anxious feelings

Resources

- shawl or cotton blanket
- mat
- lead pencil, coloured pencils or crayons
- blank paper or Worksheet 9: My Hand (see page 112)

Focus

Think about how anxiety seems to be in different places in your body.

Introduction

We may be unaware that anxiety affects our hands, as well as the rest of our bodies. Hands may feel clammy or sweaty, irritated, or always on the move. Hands may be the first indicator of anxiety as people clench and unclench them.

To Do

Sit comfortably with coloured pencils or crayons, a lead pencil, and Worksheet 9 or some blank paper nearby.

- Check that your breathing is relaxed.
- Place one hand in the centre of a page.
- Draw around your hand with the pencil.
- Think about the different sensations on your hand when you are anxious.
- Colour your hand picture to reflect these sensations.

To Think About

Hands are very important: we shake hands or use high fives, and we clap hands to show appreciation or to call on people be quiet. Try to allow your hands to be relaxed, rather than tense.

Exercise 4.2: My Anxious Hand 2

Aims

- to continue the connection between body states and anxiety
- to understand how body parts can communicate stress to other parts of the body

DOI: 10.4324/9781032256641-7

Resources

*   shawl or cotton blanket
*   mat

Focus

Think about the way you are holding your hands, and whether they are always moving or whether they become tense.

Introduction

When we are anxious, we may use both hands to clasp the back of a chair to give us the feeling that we are 'holding on'. We may also clasp our hands together and suddenly realise they are very tense, then unclench them.

To Do

Sit or lie down in a relaxed position.

*   Check that your breathing is relaxed.
*   Clasp both your hands and press them together to feel the tension.
*   Take a deep breath in, and as you breathe out, let go of your hands so they slip apart.
*   Repeat the exercise, and notice the difference between clenched hands and relaxed hands.
*   Remind yourself to sit with relaxed hands whenever you are sitting down.

To Think About

When we have got into the habit of body tension, it takes a while to get out if it. Try to be aware of when you clench your hands tight, and always try to relax your breathing with an in-out breath.

Exercise 4.3: The Iron Fist in the Velvet Glove

Aims

*   to recognise when our hands are giving double messages
*   to reassure ourselves that we don't have to keep our fists at the ready

Resources

*   shawl or cotton blanket
*   mat

Focus

Concentrate on both your hands, and be aware of how they can change in tension.

Introduction

The expression 'the iron fist in the velvet glove' illustrates how there can be a duality in our hands: we may feel relaxed, but there is an inner tension that can't let go of the clenched fist. We need to be aware of our tendency to keep our hands tense.

To Do

Sit quietly, and practise calm breathing.

*   Wrap one hand round the other, but keep the outside hand relaxed and the inside hand very tense.
*   Change the two hands around.
*   Tense both of them.

- Change them again so they are both relaxed.
- Be aware of how those states can change in different hands.

To Think About

A lot of attention needs to be focused on our hands because they are so often the clue to the initial stages of anxiety. We can practise relaxing our hands wherever we are and whatever we are doing.

Exercise 4.4: Soothing Hands

Aims

- to develop a sense of soothing in our hands
- to be aware of different hand sensations

Resources

- shawl or cotton blanket
- mat
- good-quality non-perfumed hand cream

Focus

Be aware of how easy it is for our hands to get rough and dry.

Introduction

Years ago, it was thought that moisturising creams were very much for women, and part of being feminine. However, now the use of moisturisers can be acceptable for both men and women. Using hand cream can be very self-soothing and nurturing.

To Do

Sit comfortably, and practise calm breathing.

- Feel the texture of both your hands, back and front.
- Squeeze out a small amount of hand cream, and rub it into your palms.
- Use one hand to rub the cream into the back of the other hand.
- Lace your fingers together, and make sure the cream has spread over all your palms and fingers.
- If there is any surplus cream, rub it into your cheeks so that your hands are not sticky.

To Think About

We need to be aware of how anxiety often leads to dryness of our skin, especially in our hands, our neck, and our face. Where possible, use moisturiser to improve skin texture. We need to remember that keeping hydrated also helps to avoid dry skin.

Exercise 4.5: Wrinkled Foreheads

Aims

- to continue raising awareness of different parts of the body reflecting anxiety
- to encourage self-awareness of how anxiety can increase tense body states

Resources

- shawl or cotton blanket
- mat

Focus

Pay attention to different areas of your face, especially your forehead.

Introduction

We often show tension in our faces, especially our foreheads, without being aware of it. People can get quite alarmed when others frown at them, but the frown may be an indication of anxiety rather than negativity.

To Do

Sit comfortably, and practise calm breathing.

- Practise frowning up and then frowning down.
- Using both hands, smooth away any frowning in your forehead.
- On each side of your forehead, use circular movements to relax the head muscles.
- Focus on your forehead, and be aware of how you often frown without realising it.
- Take a deep breath in, and let go of any tension in your face.

To Think About

It is very easy when we are tense to get into habits of frowning or setting our jaw in a tense way or screwing our eyes up. Try to pay attention to your whole face, and be aware of which parts of it are prone to tension.

Exercise 4.6: Pulling Faces

Aims

- to show how exaggerating movement can help get rid of tension
- to become aware of muscles we didn't know existed

Resources

- shawl or cotton blanket
- mat
- crayons or coloured pens
- Worksheet 10: Silly and Funny Faces (see page 113) and Worksheet 12: Different Facial Expressions (Cartoon Faces) (see page 115)

Focus

Try to imagine any exaggerated expressions you find amusing to look at.

Introduction

Sometimes, we become too serious when we try to relax, and end up tenser. Being a bit more light-hearted and thinking of funny expressions can be a way of reducing tension.

To Do

Sit comfortably, and practise calm breathing with Worksheets 10 and 12 and coloured pens or crayons nearby.

- Purse your lips very strongly, push them forwards, then open your mouth with a very big yawn, screw your eyes up at the same time, then relax.
- Blow out your cheeks with as much air as possible, then clap them with your hands so that they burst.
- Imitate the faces on the worksheet as closely as you can.
- Colour some of the faces on the worksheets that you find funny.
- Be aware of how your face muscles have changed from the exercises.

To Think About

We can learn to relax by stretching muscles. In particular, it is very easy to hold on to facial tension without realising it. By pulling silly faces, we can let go of deeper tension.

Exercise 4.7: Hands and Knees

Aims

- to show how our hands can be helpful to relax other tensions
- to show how we hold tension in different parts of our bodies

Resources

- shawl or cotton blanket
- mat

Focus

Sitting calmly, being aware of both of our knees.

Introduction

Tension can often be carried in our knees, and they are more difficult to relax because we use them for walking etc. We need to try to let go of tension in our knees when we are sitting or lying quietly.

To Do

Sit comfortably, and practise calm breathing.

- As you sit, place your hands on your knees.
- Are they relaxed, or are they tense?
- Use your hands to massage your knee caps with circular movements.
- Place your fingers behind your knees, and use circular movements to relax the muscles.
- Using alternate legs, just swing the knee forward and back several times.

To Think About

In later life, knees are one of the first things to show damage. It is helpful to learn to relax them when we are younger. Massaging our knees and relaxing them after sport or long exercise will help to preserve our knee health.

Exercise 4.8: Putting Your Foot in It

Aims

- to understand the potential connection between body metaphor and body state
- to encourage greater awareness of the tension in our feet

Resources

- shawl or cotton blanket
- mat

Focus

Move your concentration to your feet, and notice whether they are tense.

Introduction

The metaphor 'to put your foot in it' may stop us doing something in case we get it wrong. Getting things wrong is a frequent fear for many children and teenagers. If we take care of our feet in a literal way, it may give us the confidence to 'step out'. You may recall there was a musical called *Stepping Out* in which some older women took up tap dancing!

To Do

Sit comfortably, and practise calm breathing.

- Focus on your feet, and see if they are held in tension.
- Notice how some people will repeatedly kick their legs up and down.
- Press both your feet onto the floor up to your toes, slowly put them down again, then repeat.
- With alternate feet, circle the ankle in both directions. Be aware that your ankles, feet, and toes can be relaxed when you are sitting down.
- Reflect on the expression 'put your foot in it'.

To Think About

The famous song 'These Boots Were Made for Walking' draws our attention to the importance of our feet. If we keep our feet in a state of tension, it can cause cramps and numbness. Foot exercise can help to keep them supple and increase our confidence to 'step out'.

Exercise 4.9: My Stomach Is Churning

Aims

- to try to alleviate the anxiety that may be carried in the stomach
- to understand how the stomach may be the centre of other body tension

Resources

- shawl or cotton blanket
- mat

Focus

Be aware of your stomach and any movement or tension that it has.

Introduction

There are many expressions that communicate about tension in our stomachs. We talk about our stomach churning or feeling butterflies or the pit of our stomach dropping. All of these indicate how our stomach can be the centre of our body tension. Recent research suggests that we have a second brain in our stomachs.

To Do

Sit comfortably, and practise calm breathing.

- Place one hand on your stomach.
- Carefully breathe in through your nose, and feel your hand being pushed away by your stomach.
- Blow the air out again, and feel your hand go back.
- Notice how deep breathing can help to control any anxiety in our stomach.
- Take another deep breath, and expand your stomach as far as it will go.
- Blow the air out, and feel your stomach completely relax.

To Think About

Our stomach usually tenses up when we start to breathe in a more shallow way. By practising deep breathing in the abdomen, we can actually dispel stomach anxiety. Remember that 'stomach breathing' can change feelings, and 'rib breathing' can give us confidence.

Exercise 4.10: Breathing Out Tension

Aims

- to understand how we carry tension in our chest which can affect our breathing
- to regulate our breathing pattern in order for our rib cage to function with our lungs

Resources

- shawl or cotton blanket
- mat

Focus

Focus on your breathing pattern and how your chest expands and retracts

Introduction

When we breathe without holding in our stomach muscles, the breath comes and goes without control. When we hold in our stomach muscles, we can breathe with our upper body, expanding our rib cage. We then need to avoid tension in the shoulders and the neck.

To Do

Sit comfortably, and focus on your breathing patterns.

- Hold your stomach muscles slightly in.
- Breathe in, and notice your rib cage expanding.
- Notice how your lungs are full of air and need more room!
- Blow the air out, and notice how your rib cage contracts.
- Try to establish an easy pattern of breathing in and out with the rib cage.

To Think About

When we learn to breathe with our rib cage, we learn to expand our breathing capacity. The more deep breathing we do, the more relaxed we will become. However, if we are tense in the chest area, we will also be tense in our necks and shoulders.

CBT Exercises

1. Sit in an upright chair, and close your eyes if it feels comfortable. Scan your whole body, and see where you feel tense. Take a deep breath, and try to relax any tense areas.
2. You need coloured pens and paper. Draw an outline of a body. Colour any areas where you feel any tension. Try and relax them with deep breathing.

Working Online

These exercises can be applied online with individuals and groups. Variations can include: running around the room and stopping, stopping and make a shape, and stopping and making a sound.

Summary

We have begun to focus on various body parts as well as our whole body. We have explored metaphors about our bodies such as 'putting your foot in it' or 'my stomach is churning'. We are continuing to emphasise the importance of relaxing tension and how it can all be changed by breathing.

Questions and Reflections for Discussion

1. If you scan your own body, what areas are usually tense?
2. Do you remember being tense as a child? Was it about anything in particular?
3. You notice that a teenager coming to see you always sits on her hands – how might you explore this situation?
4. What can we learn from children having tension in their shoulders or their hands?
5. A child in the class is always tapping his foot – what might this mean?

Chapter 5

Facial Expressions and Feelings

We can easily be affected by the facial expressions of other people. A 'chance glance' can reduce us to quivers. People who communicate nothing with their faces can be even more unnerving. As social beings, we need feedback from others in terms of how they are feeling. Paul Ekman contributed seminal research on how we express emotions through our faces and the fact that many of these expressions are universal, such as contempt, anger, disgust, fear, sadness, surprise, and joy (see Ekman 2003 and 2004/2007).

Exercise 5.1: Facial Expressions 1

Aims

- to develop greater awareness of mindfulness
- to develop ideas of feelings and facial expressions

Resources

- shawl or cotton blanket
- mat

Focus

Think about people for whom you have positive feelings.

Introduction

It is often difficult when we are anxious to have positive thoughts and feelings. This exercise encourages people to have positive thoughts about someone specific. This usually means it is easier to reduce anxiety.

To Do

Sit or lie comfortably on your mat with your blanket or shawl.

- Allow your mind to focus on another person you feel is kind.
- Picture that person's face, and look at their expression.
- Are they usually smiley, or serious?
- Try having that expression yourself, and see how it feels.
- Be aware of how it compares with your own day-to-day expression.

To Think About

Think about how changing your facial expressions can change your feelings. We need to be aware of people's facial expressions and how they may give some indication of their mood. However, they may also be feeling tense.

DOI: 10.4324/9781032256641-8

Exercise 5.2: Facial Expressions 2

Aims

- to develop greater awareness of facial expressions
- to understand how changing expressions can change moods

Resources

- shawl or cotton blanket
- mat

Focus

Concentrate on changes in facial expressions and how they affect us.

Introduction

Moods can be changed by altering facial expressions, and facial expressions can be changed by altering our mood. Think about how actors are able to do it. By practising these changes, we start to gain greater control.

To Do

Sit or lie down comfortably, with your shawl or blanket wrapped around you if you wish.

- Close your eyes, if it feels comfortable, and breathe calmly.
- Think about some of the common moods people may be feeling.
- Imagine how it affects their facial expressions.
- Allow yourself to feel different facial expressions, even making funny faces.
- Finish with a smiley face or funny face that does not provoke anxiety.

To Think About

If we change our facial expression, does it change the feeling inside? We can try practising those expressions and see if our mood changes. Maintaining an expression of calm or pleasure may enable us to feel less anxious.

Exercise 5.3: Faces and Feelings

Aims

- to differentiate between different facial expressions and how they make us feel
- to be aware of our own facial expressions and the impact they have on other people

Resources

- shawl or cotton blanket
- mat or chair and table
- coloured pens or crayons
- Worksheet 11: Different Facial Expressions (see page 114)

Introduction

When we are anxious, we often stop differentiating between facial expressions, and everyone may be perceived as hostile and unfriendly. Using a worksheet with many different expressions on it, we can start to distinguish between different expressions and feelings.

To Do

Sitting in a comfortable position on the floor or at the table with Worksheet 11 nearby, check your breathing.

- Close your eyes, and imagine the faces of all the people you see around you.
- Open your eyes, and look at worksheet 11, which shows faces with many different expressions.
- Colour in the faces that have meaning for you, but don't allow yourself to choose more negative than positive ones.
- Out of all the faces, choose one that is the most positive, and colour it with a lot more detail.
- Is this the face of someone in particular? Could it be you?

To Think About

We can allow ourselves to imagine positive expressions in other people and practise the expressions ourselves. We should always end with a positive expression, whether it is smiling, laughing, content, calm, or happy – or maybe it is more than one of these?

Exercise 5.4: Voices in My Head

Aims

- to evolve strategies to ignore negative voices in our heads
- to encourage internal positive voices to replace the negative ones

Resources

- shawl or cotton blanket
- mat

Focus

Think about voices we hear, both inside our heads as well as those in everyday life.

Introduction

Many of us who are anxious experience negative voices inside our heads. These voices may tell us we are useless, worthless, nobody likes us, or we are no good at anything. This exercise aims to start switching off the negative voices.

To Do

Sit calmly, and focus on your breathing.

- Bring to mind a negative voice you sometimes experience.
- Is it about how you look, what you do, what you achieve?
- Try to let go of the negative voice by saying the opposite, so that a voice that says, 'you look awful' is now saying 'you look great'.
- Repeat the positive statement in your head several times.
- Give a large sigh.

To Think About

When we have negative voices inside our heads, it is often difficult to counter them. Some may have been around for a long time. Gradually replacing the negative ones with positive ones helps to reduce our anxiety and to build a positive self-image

Exercise 5.5: Calming Sounds and Rhythms

Aims

- to raise awareness of music or singing that has a soothing effect
- to be aware of the rhythmic nature of songs and chants which have a calming impact

Resources

- shawl or cotton blanket
- mat

Focus

Call to mind any pieces of music that you find calming and are able to listen to more than once.

Introduction

Many of us who feel anxious have jangly sounds inside our heads. It can be a very spiky feeling. Encouraging increased awareness of soothing music and song can help to diffuse the jaggedness and enable us to feel more relaxed.

To Do

Sit calmly, and breathe evenly.

- Think about different types of music and the effect they have on your mood.
- Choose one piece of music you feel is calming, and imagine you can hear it right now.
- Is it a popular song or a piece of classical music or a children's song you can remember, or something else?
- Try to recall the very first time you heard this music.
- Remember that this calming music can be recalled whenever you get anxious.

To Think About

Different types of music can be exciting and stimulating or soothing and calming. Generally speaking, music with a regular rhythm is more calming than a random rhythm.

Apparently, Mozart is supposed to be the most soothing music to play during pregnancy, childbirth, and after babies are born.

Exercise 5.6: Positive and Negative Images

Aims

- to further develop a balance between positive and negatives views on life
- to develop insight into pictures that may carry our various feelings

Resources

- shawl or cotton blanket
- mat
- coloured pens or crayons
- blank paper

Focus

Trying to keep a balance between positive and negative images.

Introduction

When we suffer from anxiety, many of us have a greater proportion of negative feelings about other people than positive ones. This exercise will try to balance the negative and positive images by creating new images.

To Do

Sit on your mat with paper and coloured pens or crayons nearby. Before you start the exercise, close your eyes and breathe deeply to help you focus.

- Think about a situation or a person that feels very negative to you.
- Make scribbles or random lines on one sheet of paper that convey your negative feelings.
- Continue to breathe deeply, and think of a positive person or place.
- Using colours, create positive shapes and patterns on another sheet of paper.
- Put the two sheets of paper side by side, and look at the contrast in shape and colour.

To Think About

It is very easy for us to allow the negative to take over from the positive. Think about where negative feelings come from, as we are certainly not born with them. However, babies and small children pick up very quickly on negative feelings from others.

Exercise 5.7: The Face in the Nightmare

Aims

- to bring dreams into the communication and acknowledge their importance
- to address issues of fear in 'bad dreams'

Resources

- shawl or cotton blanket
- mat
- coloured pens or crayons
- blank paper

Focus

Allow yourself to recall a bad dream and a scary face from the dream (if you get anxious, remember to breathe calmly).

Introduction

This exercise begins to test our control of scary experiences. Rather than being frightened of nightmares, we can start to understand them. Some people keep themselves awake because they are scared of nightmares.

To Do

Sit on your mat, wrap your shawl or blanket around yourself if you wish, breathe calmly, and have coloured pens or crayons and paper nearby.

- Recall the scary face from the dream.
- Draw it in as much detail as possible.
- If this face was in a film, what would the story be?
- Draw a 'good' face that overcomes the scary one.
- Remember the film with its conclusion instead of the dream.

To Think About

Often, we can get trapped in a dream sequence and imagine it is real. Dreams are like films that tell us a story. We should always try to find the story in the dream and make sure it has an ending.

Exercise 5.8: Masks and Clowns

Aims

- to differentiate between the mask and the face
- to highlight anxiety about some types of 'mask'

Resources

- shawl or cotton blanket
- mat
- coloured pens or crayons
- blank paper

Focus

Think about the faces of clowns or other characters that may be scary.

Introduction

As adults, we often assume that 'larger-than-life' characters are fun or endearing for children. However, a clown or a traditionally costumed Father Christmas may bring terror, or at least worry, to some children. In this case, saying 'Don't be silly' is not an option!

To Do

Sit comfortably, with coloured pens or crayons and paper nearby.

- Close your eyes if it feels OK, and think about faces of characters that may be scary – perhaps clowns, fairground characters, or Santa Claus.
- Can you recall any scary faces when you were younger?
- If so, draw one of the faces in one corner of the paper, making it small.
- Draw a larger face which is not scary that you like.
- Compare the two, and make sure the second face is larger than the first.

To Think About

Large faces that are much bigger than a child can be very scary, although adults may assume they are fun. We need to approach new images in entertainment or carnivals with caution until small children have some practice at responding without fear.

Exercise 5.9: The Friendly Face – Mine!

Aims

- to encourage participants to let go of negative feelings about themselves
- to develop a positive and friendly image that they can own

Resources

- shawl or cotton blanket
- mat

Focus

Reflect on the friendly face of someone else, and be clear about the detail.

Introduction

Part of the underlying causes of social anxiety is the belief that other people think badly about us and want to criticise us. By recalling a friendly face, we may be able to take on that face ourselves. A friendly face in our lives can lead to very positive feelings.

To Do

Sit comfortably, and breathe calmly.

- Reflect on friendly and unfriendly faces, kind and unkind.
- Bring to mind someone friendly in your life you have great respect for.
- Think about the kindness in this person's face.
- Try to imitate the expression yourself.
- Practise internalising the qualities that come from this kind of face.

To Think About

We need to rethink the thoughts in our minds about kind and unkind people. We need to try to focus more on the kind faces and practise these faces ourselves. How do our feelings change inside when we change our own facial expressions?

CBT Exercises

1. Cut out some cartoon faces from a magazine and label the feelings being expressed.
2. Copy those expressions yourself, and see if your feelings change when you change your facial expression.

Working Online

Care must be taken when using these techniques online, as some of the experiences are scary. Discuss with parents whether they could join in and do the exercises together with their children. If the child or young person is not happy with this, then make sure a parent will be available if they find the session becomes scary. Always emphasise with parents that fear and anxiety must be taken seriously.

Summary

We have explored the impact different faces can have on us, and the fact that sometimes it can be really scary. We have discussed faces that appear in our nightmares and how we can take control of these feelings. We have practised choosing kind faces and imitating their expressions ourselves.

Questions and Reflections for Discussion

1. Think about your own fears as a child.
2. Were you able to tell someone when you were scared?
3. Remember that some children disguise fear with aggression.
4. Do you have open discussions about dreams and nightmares with clients and pupils?
5. Can you remember someone in your life who was kind? Try asking the same question in your groups or with individuals.

Chapter 6

Where Is My Safe Place?

Safety is something that is experienced by our bodies, rather than a cognitive evaluation. There may be facts that we know about the safety of a place or a person, but it is how we feel, rather than how we think, that will convince us. Stephen Porges says:

> Safety is associated with different environmental features when defined by bodily responses versus cognitive evaluations. In a critical sense, when it comes to identifying safety from an adaptive survival perspective, the "wisdom" resides in our body and in the structures of our nervous system that function outside the realm of awareness.
>
> (Porges 2017, p.43)

This, of course, means that we need to have some flexibility when we apply CBT principles to learning and therapy, and need to incorporate both body and brain exercises.

Exercise 6.1: I Do Not Feel Safe (Indoors)

Aims

- to identify an unsafe place that causes anxiety
- to name any fears associated with the place

Resources

- shawl or cotton blanket
- mat

Focus

Think about several spaces indoors, choosing the one that feels most scary.

Introduction

Buildings have atmospheres, and some places may feel spookier than others. A space in a house, or several, may have feelings attached to them. Maybe something happened in that space, or the light may be dim so it seems scary. It is important to accept these feelings instead of dismissing them as silly.

To Do

Sit comfortably, and establish regular, rhythmic breathing.

- Concentrate on a space indoors that feels scary
- How old were you when you noticed it?
- Do you know why, or is it a feeling or an atmosphere?
- Breathe more deeply, and think of all the detail of this space.
- Imagine blowing purifying air into this space to cleanse it: actually blow this air as you breathe in through your nose and out through your mouth.

DOI: 10.4324/9781032256641-9

To Think About

It is unhelpful to dismiss people's fears and anxieties. I know a very intelligent woman who told me how unhappy she was in her house. She was convinced the previous owner had put a curse on the house and that the curse would not allow her to settle down. It was a very beautiful house with a rose garden she created, but always at the back of her mind was the feeling of the curse.

Exercise 6.2: I Do Not Feel Safe (Outdoors)

Aims

- to raise awareness of the reality that some spaces outside are scary
- to externalise and address fears that may be imagined or real

Resources

- shawl or cotton blanket
- mat

Focus

Bring to mind any anxiety that happens outside when you walk through particular places.

Introduction

It is unpleasant for many people to walk through unlit spaces such as alleyways or lanes, or to have to travel through hallways or in lifts late at night. There can be real dangers in these places, and we need to evolve a code of safe journeys for everyone, not just children or teenagers.

To Do

Sit comfortably, and breathe in through your nose and blow out through your mouth.

- Allow your mind to wander freely over outside space where you live.
- Then do so further away, perhaps near school or college or shops.
- Be aware when you become tense in any particular space.
- Mark that space in your mind as a place where you feel anxious.
- Reflect on whether this space is dangerous (unlit, violent crime) or feels like it could be dangerous.

To Think About

Encourage people to pay attention to spaces that feel unsafe. Suggest that young people walk in groups, carry torches, and let adults know where they are. Reassurance is very important, and perhaps we should think about providing more community support.

Exercise 6.3: I Need to Avoid (Water)

Aims

- to understand that fear of water can have its roots in early childhood
- to develop a feeling that water can be playful and fun

Resources

- the opportunity to be outdoors with access to water (a pool or a tap)

Focus

Consider whether all water is scary, or just larger quantities, such as lakes or seas.

Introduction

Fear of water is not uncommon, and some people make connections through the technique of dipping new-born babies who are not breathing in bowls of hot and cold water to make them gasp. People may be pushed into swimming pools or encounter huge waves that have caused a sense of drowning. Encouraging children and teenagers to have fun with small, controllable amounts of water can help to diminish their anxiety.

To Do

Walk around outside, and notice the landscape. Remember to breathe calmly.

*   Notice where there is water outside – maybe a tap or puddles after rain.
*   Fill a small can of water from the tap, and splash it with your fingers.
*   If there are flower beds, use the water in the can to water the plants.
*   If it feels OK, use a larger bowl and splash water with both hands before watering the garden.
*   Use a hosepipe or large watering can to water plants, trees, and hedges, and feel in control of the water.

To Think About

Because we live in water for nine months before we are born, water can be the most playful element, and can be associated with wet sand and mud pies. It can also be awe-inspiring in lakes, waterfalls, rivers, and seascapes. However, for people who are frightened of water, it can lead to one fear after another unless we are able to bring about change.

Exercise 6.4: I Need to Avoid (Fire)

Aims

*   to bring about a gentle introduction to fire
*   to show contrasting facets of fire that may balance the fear

Resources

*   shawl or cotton blanket
*   LED tea lights

Focus

Be aware of how your breathing changes when you think of situations involving fire or a flame.

Introduction

Fear of fire comes in many forms: we may have been burnt as a child, a relative may have been killed in a house fire, or we may have witnessed a fire that was out of control. These quite contrasting examples can cause long-term fear and anxiety about fire. It can reduce celebrations such as birthdays, with celebratory candles, to times of high anxiety

To Do

Sit comfortably, and breathe calmly in through your nose and out through your mouth.

*   Bring to mind one very small flame, such as a tea light in a burner of essential oil.
*   Imagine the smell of lavender or rosemary coming from the burner.
*   Have a big stretch, and check that your breathing has stayed calm.
*   Take a LED tea light, switch it on, and focus on it.
*   Be aware of whether your anxiety increases or not.

To Think About

Fear of fire is a very deep-rooted feeling which may have origins in our distant past when fires could easily get out of control. When individuals have additional fears, it is important that they are addressed gradually in a supportive atmosphere.

Exercise 6.5: I Need to Avoid (Fire 2)

Aims

- to structure fire fears into a form that has a resolution and control
- to develop the use of stories about fire to bring about distancing

Resources

- shawl or cotton blanket
- mat
- Story Sheet 5: Fetching the Fire from the Underworld (see page 138)

Focus

Reflect on stories that have a theme of fire, especially where it is a positive force.

Introduction

There are many myths and stories about the elements, especially fire. They include the time when people did not have fire and had to discover it or steal it. If we use stories where fire is a positive element, it can help to re-structure fears and panics about fire. Read the story calmly, and be mindful of any anxiety, then stop reading and encourage deep breathing. People can also be encouraged to research stories for themselves.

To Do

Sit or lie down comfortably to listen to the story.

- 'Fetching the Fire from the Underworld' is an ancient story about a community that had no fire.
- They were miserable and cold, and unable to cook their food.
- Listen to the story while remembering your breathing.
- Be aware if at any time you get anxious.
- Reflect on the story, and notice if you were able to stay calm.

To Think About

This story helps us to re-think fire as something necessary and important. The characters are encouraged to be generous with fire and share it with their neighbours. There are also humorous characters, such as the little devils chasing the pig, to lighten the tone.

Exercise 6.6: I Feel Safe Where? (1)

Aims

- to encourage people to identify a place that feels safe
- to develop the capacity to name the 'elements' of safety

Resources

- shawl or cotton blanket
- mat
- crayons or coloured pens
- blank paper

Focus

Think about the spaces that don't make us feel anxious.

Introduction

Spaces can cause anxiety if they are unknown. They can also create worries if something unexpected or unpleasant has happened there before. Unfortunately, with the growth of smartphone use, filming of shock reactions when people are scared is quite common.

To Do

Sit comfortably and breathe easily, with crayons or coloured pens and paper nearby.

- Let your mind roam across any safe place you remember from the past.
- Leave out any places where you were scared because you were hiding from something or someone.
- Focus on the best one of all, wherever it was.
- Draw this safe place to fill the whole sheet of paper, include anything else that was nearby, such as trees or fields, and colour it in.
- Try to fix this place in your memory – look at your picture, and remember all the details.

To Think About

Everyone has places where they feel safe and calm. If we are subject to danger or unpleasantness, we may feel we are hiding, but may still be anxious. It's important to have a safe place where we know we are safe. Many children who come to play therapy first create a safe place with a play-tent or a blanket over chairs.

Exercise 6.7: I Feel Safe Where? (2)

Aims

- to further encourage people to identify a place that feels safe
- to develop the capacity to differentiate the safe place from the hiding place

Resources

- shawl or cotton blanket
- mat
- modelling clay or plasticine

Focus

Create more pictures in your head of safe places rather than hiding places.

Introduction

Safe spaces are different from hiding places where we go when we are scared. We can hide behind a hoodie or a peaked cap, or both! A safe space is somewhere where we know there is no intrusion and we can sit calmly and breathe normally.

To Do

Sit comfortably, with modelling clay or plasticine nearby.

- Let your mind recall any safe places you remember from the past – maybe there was just one.
- Leave out any places where you were scared and hid from something or someone.
- While remembering, have the clay in your hands and start to mould it.
- Use the clay to create the special place with as much detail as possible.
- Try to fix this place in your memory, and recall all the details.

To Think About

Everyone needs a place where they feel safe and calm. In some situations, such as war or flood or where there is domestic violence, it may feel that nowhere is safe. It will take time and persistence to be able to create a safe place in our imagination if there is nowhere available in the outside world, or it may feel like there is nowhere that can provide us with safety.

Exercise 6.8: I Feel Safe Where? (3)

Aims

- to further encourage people to construct a place that feels protective
- to stimulate the imagination with the details of the safe place

Resources

- shawl or cotton blanket
- mat
- collage materials – large sheets of paper and a selection from scraps of coloured paper and fabric, tissue paper, recycled stuff, wool, string, white glue, scissors, paints, and brushes

Focus

Think in greater detail of a special safe place – maybe it does not exist yet!

Introduction

Sometimes, we need to imagine a place that is safe and think about the different elements that make it safe. Once we can imagine it, we can make it, and feel more secure as a result. We will then have a safe place that cannot be taken away from us.

To Do

Sit comfortably, with the collage materials nearby.

- You can choose a safe place that you know exists, or you can imagine one that would be the perfect place to feel safe in.
- It could be somewhere crazy – a treehouse, or your own island?
- Use the collage materials to create this place.
- Paint any extra detail you wish to have in the collage.
- Maybe photograph your collage so you can always recall the picture.

To Think About

We can use our imagination to create a special place. This enables us to really stretch our creativity and make a place that may be exotic, fantastic, or totally unrealistic! Places created through collage may have a temporary life-span, but they can be photographed and saved and used as reminders when the going gets tough.

Exercise 6.9: I Feel Safe Where? (4)

Aims

- to further encourage people to create safety through their imagination
- to encourage control of images that feed feelings of safety

Resources

- shawl or cotton blanket
- mat

Focus

Think in greater detail of another special safe place – maybe it has not existed until now!

Introduction

Sometimes, we can just imagine a new place that is safe. We can think about the detail and what is important, both inside and outside. Does it have a real location in the world, or is everything in the imagination? It takes time to be able to create without concrete images or materials.

To Do

Sit comfortably, and breathe calmly.

- Start by imagining a new safe place.
- This is a space you are creating from the beginning, so think about colours, textures, etc.
- You have absolute freedom to put in it whatever you wish, both inside and outside.
- You can change or adapt elements in it – try them out and test them.
- End up with a final place that feels OK, where you feel calm and positive.

To Think About

Once we can use our imagination to create a safe space, we can start to have control over our anxieties. Anxious thoughts may decrease and no longer invade our waking moments or continuously bombard us with messages. Eventually, these changes will make a difference to our anxiety in everyday life. However, we all have places to go to get away from today's moments – it's called day-dreaming!

Exercise 6.10: Journey to a Safe Place

Aims

- to enable people to journey to a place of safety of their own choosing
- to vocalise elements in the journey that are reassuring and nurturing

Resources

- shawl or cotton blanket
- mat
- coloured pens or crayons
- blank paper
- Story Sheet 8: Journey to a Safe Place (see page 141)

Focus

Free your mind to go on a journey of discovery.

Introduction

It can be helpful with any age group to go on an imaginary journey in order to get to a safe place. We call this type of activity 'creative visualisation', and the journey can be the preparation for arriving at our destination. We are given choices about the elements we would like in our safe place. There is an emphasis on growth, in contrast to anxiety, which often holds us fast and stops us from moving.

To Do

Sit comfortably and breathe calmly, with coloured pens or crayons and paper nearby.

- Imagine you are going on a journey to a safe place. Where will it start? It could be in a garden, the street, or wherever you choose to be the beginning. Remember that the journey is safe, like your destination.

- What is the path you are following? Is it rough or smooth, straight or bendy?
- What sort of landscape does the path pass through? Are there any woods or fields, or sand and sea?
- How is the light on this journey – light and sunny, or dark and cloudy? Are there shadows?
- Arrive at your safe place and go inside, making sure the door or covering is in place so you are completely private. Spend as much time there as you wish.
- Return along the path you came, remembering all the detail until you arrive where you started.
- If you wish, draw a picture of your safe place.

To Think About

Once we have created the 'Journey to a Safe Place' in our imagination, with or without drawing a picture, we can return to it any time we wish. Initially, we may get anxious about creating the detail, in which case the story sheet is available to help us along.

CBT Exercises

1. Try to describe how your body feels when you don't feel safe. Think of ways you can change the negative feelings to positive feelings.
2. Breathe deeply, and remember how your breathing can change your bodily feelings.

Working Online

These exercises can be developed online, and individuals and groups may feel safer when they are working that way. It is important to have a sense of feeling safe in the online setting. It is helpful if parents can also be involved and contribute to the feelings of safety wherever the session is taking place. It is very important that parents take their child's feelings about lack of safety seriously.

Summary

We have described places that feel safe and those that don't feel safe, as well as elements like water and fire that may create anxiety. We have looked at creating safe places in our imagination and finding ways to make 'the journey to a safe place' which will gradually build up our confidence. We have used a story sheets to guide us on the journey.

Questions and Reflections for Discussion

1. Think about your own childhood and feelings of safety.
2. How would you manage pupils who hide under desks or in cupboards?
3. Do you work with children who seem constantly anxious at school or in therapy?
4. How would you deal with a young person who constantly leaves the session as soon as you have greeted them?
5. What would your response be to parents who insist on knowing the contents of your sessions?

Summary of Part II

This part of the book has addressed issues of lack of safety for children and young people. It is apparent that many of them have physical symptoms as a way of expressing their worries and anxieties. It is important that parents, teachers, and therapists take the fears seriously and find ways to create safety and reassurance for children and young people of all ages.

Part III

Energy, Mandalas, and Stories

Introduction

There are three chapters in Part III: 'Replacing Anxiety with Energy', 'Mandalas and Mantras', and 'The Land of Stories'

Part III focuses on strategies for regaining the energy we lose when we are anxious. When we have extreme anxiety, it uses up much of our day-to-day resources. It takes enormous effort to maintain a state of anxiety, and as we know, it can also affect our daily routines. We may try to avoid situations that make us anxious, check them out several times, or refuse social engagements in an attempt to shore up our anxieties. What happens, of course, is that our anxiety increases and we use yet more energy!

We also need methods for reminding us how to deal with anxiety if it returns. All of us have some anxiety, and often when we feel we have dealt with it, we may panic that it may return unexpectedly. We can adopt special phrases to deal with the panic before it takes over, or have a special talisman in our pocket that is reassuring when we hold it. Many people still have their toys from childhood which can be cuddled when the going gets tough!

Shakespeare informs our understanding of the destructiveness of anxiety and how it can erode our confidence and wreak havoc in our lifestyle.

Anxiety could be described as an arid desert where nothing can be nurtured and grow. Small amounts of rain slowly enable growth and change, but if it is a flood, it is all too much and becomes overwhelming. I'm reminded of the beautiful quotation from Shakespeare's 'Venus and Adonis', stanza 134: 'Love comforteth like sunshine after rain'.

People sometimes describe their anxiety as flooding them, as a metaphor for being overwhelmed or drowning in their despair:

> Great floods have flown
> From simple sources.
> (Shakespeare,
> *All's Well That Ends Well*,
> Act 2, Scene i)

Others use the metaphor of the garden and weeds that are crowding out their positive flower-thoughts:

> 'Tis an unweeded garden,
> That grows to seed.
> (Shakespeare, *Hamlet*,
> Act 1, Scene ii)

Look out for the garden metaphor in Chapter 9 of this third part.

Learning Outcomes for Part III

- to explore how we dissipate energy because of anxiety
- to describe methods to deal with the return of anxiety
- to remember that Shakespeare had a profound understanding of anxiety and its destructive potential

DOI: 10.4324/9781032256641-10

Replacing Anxiety with Energy

Exercise 7.1: Banishing the Burden 1

Aims

- to enable young people to take control of their anxiety
- to facilitate a change process from 'static' to 'current'

Resources

- shawl or cotton blanket
- mat
- crayons or coloured pens
- Worksheet 14: Bricks of Ice (see page 117)

Focus

Think about how anxiety is affecting your body

Introduction

We talk about the weight of our worries and the burden of our responsibilities. Bob Dylan once said: 'Being noticed can be a burden. Jesus got himself crucified because he got himself noticed. So I disappear a lot.'

It can be easier for us not to be noticed rather than feel anxious that we are being seen, maybe judgementally.

To Do

Sit comfortably with crayons or coloured pens and Worksheet 14 nearby, and practise calm breathing – give a big sigh.

- Feel relaxed, and check that you are not holding any part of your body in tension.
- Imagine that your anxiety is like a bag of bricks weighing down your shoulders.
- Slowly, the bricks are melting as they are made of ice, so feel the cold water running down your back.
- Allow yourself to feel free of the burden, and then imagine the sun comes out and dries up the water.
- Colour Worksheet 14 with the bricks and the sun, and think about the experience.

To Think About

If we can imagine ourselves to be anxious and burdened, then we can also imagine ourselves to be free of the burden. It is important to allow ourselves the power of our imagination to bring about change. Even if it is for a moment

DOI: 10.4324/9781032256641-11

Exercise 7.2: Banishing the Burden 2

Aims

- to encourage the development of the imagination for self-help
- to focus an image on the reduction of anxiety

Resources

- shawl or cotton blanket
- mat
- rayons or coloured pens
- Worksheet 15: Sisyphus and the Rock (see page 118) and Story Sheet 6: The Myth of Sisyphus (see page 139)

Focus

Concentrate on the sheer weight of your anxiety and how it feels.

Introduction

The ancient story about Sisyphus can remind us of the ongoing nature of burdens on our shoulders. In the story, Sisyphus was a king who was punished for being vain and lying. He had to push a huge stone up a hill, when it promptly rolled all the way down again, so he had to start pushing it up the hill all over again.

To Do

Sit comfortably as you practise calm breathing, with crayons or coloured pens and Worksheet 15 and Story Sheet 6 nearby.

- Bring to mind any weight you carry on your shoulders.
- The weight on your shoulder feels very heavy. Imagine you can place it in front of you.
- In your mind, start to push it away from you.
- Now try to really push it away with your hands so it stays away – give a final big push so that it goes!
- Read through Story Sheet 6.
- Colour in Worksheet 15, and see how it feels for the stone to roll away and not return.

To Think About

So often, our burdens feel permanent and we can become unconscious of them, as though they are an essential part of our lives. All anxieties can be reduced, and some can disappear altogether if we have the strength to let them go. But it can also feel scary.

Exercise 7.3: Banishing the Burden 3

Aims

- to encourage physical solutions for reducing anxiety
- to emphasise the idea of small steps towards change

Resources

- shawl or cotton blanket
- mat
- Story Sheet 6: The Myth of Sisyphus (see page 139)

Focus

Reflect on the aches in your shoulders from carrying all this anxiety.

Introduction

Most of us get so used to carrying anxiety that we forget the impact on our bodies from the underlying tension. Getting rid of anxiety has to be gradual, but we hope permanent. Physical changes need to be gradual, or we may have increased aches and pains!

To Do

Lie on the mat with Story Sheet 6 nearby, make a pillow of the folded shawl or blanket, and establish a steady breathing pattern.

- Think about performing animals who have to spin a ball on their noses.
- Slowly raise both legs, and imagine you have a spinning ball on your feet.
- Use your foot movements to encourage the ball to spin repeatedly.
- Make a big effort, bend your knees, and push the ball as far away as you can.
- Repeat the exercise, then read through Story Sheet 6: The Myth of Sisyphus.

To Think About

Sometimes our anxiety can feel like the repetitive motions of the performing animal. Keep the ball in the air at all costs – imagine what might happen if we let it fall! Sometimes, we just need to let it fall and let go of the tension and expectation. We are not performing creatures!

Exercise 7.4: Floating Away! (1)

Aims

- to develop an alternative to pushing anxiety away – letting it float
- to use the imagination if real materials would harm the environment

Resources

- shawl or cotton blanket
- mat
- crayons or coloured pens
- Worksheet 16: The Anxiety Balloon (see page 119)

Focus

In contrast to the heavy feelings, think about anxiety being able to float away.

Introduction

It's important that we can experience contrasting feelings about our anxiety. If it can be heavy but able to roll away, as in Exercise 7.2, can it also be light and float away? Again, we need to use our imagination to help us get out of stuck feelings that are so often fuelled by anxiety.

To Do

Sit or lie down with coloured pens or crayons and Worksheet 16 nearby, and establish a calm breathing pattern.

- As you breathe calmly, imagine a large, strong balloon at the end of a string.
- The balloon has all your anxieties inside it and has your name written on it.
- As you picture it, hold on to the string as it tugs at your hand.
- It is so strong that it pulls away from your hand and floats away – see it disappearing into the distance.
- You can hear a loud bang as it explodes! Colour in Worksheet 16 to mirror your experience.

Please note that it would be inappropriate to do this exercise with a real helium-filled balloon outdoors, as the burst balloon could be ingested by an animal, possibly with fatal results.

To Think About

We use metaphors such as floating on clouds to express positive feelings. In this exercise, we can allow our anxiety to float away and hope we will feel lighter and calmer as a result. The letting go of the string is a decisive moment.

Exercise 7.5: Floating Away! (2)

Aims

- to be able to name individual anxieties and address them
- to give ourselves permission to let go of a person who causes us stress

Resources

- shawl or cotton blanket
- mat

Focus

Reflect on any person who causes you anxiety.

Introduction

It is always difficult when we experience anxiety when we are with particular people, especially if it is a member of our family. They may cause us anxiety, but we may also have other feelings towards them. I well remember a history teacher who terrified me, and if ever she looked at me, I blushed – but she taught history very well!

To Do

Lie down or sit in a relaxed position on your mat, and breathe calmly.

- Call to mind a person who causes you anxiety.
- Allow yourself to think about the person without getting stressed.
- In your imagination, paint the person's face on a large inflated balloon.
- Take a very deep breath, and blow this balloon away – use real energy.
- Take another deep breath, and make sure the balloon goes far away out of sight.

To Think About

It is helpful if we can turn breath into energy. By blowing the imaginary balloon away, we are empowering ourselves to address the situation. We are not trying to destroy the person. Rather, we are distancing ourselves from them by using our own energy

Exercise 7.6: Floating Away! (3)

Aims

- to establish our imagination as an agent of change
- to develop the confidence to control our anxiety through our imagination

Resources

- shawl or cotton blanket
- mat
- crayons or coloured pens
- blank paper
- Worksheet 17: Dancing Demons (see page 120)

Focus

Allow your imagination to be flexible to bring about change.

Introduction

The exercises earlier in this book are intended to develop some confidence in individuals to take greater charge of their imagination. Instead of imagining terrible things that might go wrong, we want to try to imagine things that could go right. Instead of feeling it would be useless to try something out, let's encourage ourselves to consider that it might just be useful.

To Do

Sit comfortably with crayons or coloured pens and paper and Worksheet 17 nearby, and establish calm breathing.

- Bring to mind one of your anxious feelings; give it a shape and a colour.
- Try to imagine that the picture is in fact a demon.
- As you picture it, imagine it getting smaller and smaller.
- When it becomes really small, allow it to dance away into the distance.
- Choose one of the demons to colour in on Worksheet 17.

To Think About

Small children can imagine scary monsters that are bigger than themselves. As we get older, the monsters often change into feelings and anxieties. We can control them by allowing them to become insignificant through our imagination.

Exercise 7.7: Creative Visualisation I

Aims

- to build on the skills of the imagination
- to bring about change through the imagination

Resources

- shawl or cotton blanket
- mat

Focus

Give permission to your imagination to allow you to go on a journey.

Introduction

Creative visualisation is a method that can allow us to literally travel with our imagination. It is similar to daydreaming, but has a specific structure with a beginning, middle, and end. It allows our imagination to wander into new territory and discover new ideas and places.

To Do

Sit calmly, and breathe in through your nose and out through your mouth.

- Focus on the image of a path you would like to follow – is it straight or curvy?
- Imagine you are walking along the path, the sun is shining, and you are crossing a field.
- When you get to the other side, decide whether to go through the woods or take the path that goes around the woods.
- Follow the path of your choice, and there in front of you is something very special – what a lovely surprise!
- Stand still for a few moments, taking in every bit of detail.

- Now it's time to return along the same path until you get back to where you started.

To Think About

Learning how to travel on an imaginary journey helps to diminish anxiety. In this exercise, we are told very little about the journey apart from the fact that it is positive and we have choices. Then we find something along the way that is a special surprise! This is one of the simplest creative visualisation exercises that allows us to let go of current anxiety and discover something new.

Exercise 7.8: Creative Visualisation 2

Aims

- to strengthen our capacity to allow change
- to use the imagination to move forward in this change

Resources

- shawl or cotton blanket
- mat
- crayons or coloured pens
- Worksheet 18: The Tree of Worries (see page 121) and Story Sheet 7: The Golden Bird of Burdens (see page 140)

Focus

Try to imagine your anxieties in little parcels, labelled, and tied with string.

Introduction

Anxieties can feel as if they are piling up so they overwhelm us. It can help if we can create smaller parcels of them rather than one huge burden. Once we start this dissection process, each part becomes less powerful, and we can try to make them mobile. We can move them around so they become less of a burden.

To Do

Sit comfortably with crayons or coloured pens and Worksheet 18 and Story Sheet 7 nearby, and breathe in a calm way.

- Imagine you are following the path across the field – the journey is slow because you are carrying a number of your worries.
- Your shoulders feel heavy with the weight, and you are distracted from the lovely things around you.
- On the other side of the field, you see an ancient and large tree with enormous branches, and as you get nearer, you see small bundles tied to the branches.
- Take all your worries, and tie them individually to the branches – you begin to feel lighter and lighter. You almost skip home again!
- Use Worksheet 18 to colour in your ideas of the Worry Tree, then read Story Sheet 7: The Golden Bird of Burdens.

To Think About

The idea of a worry tree that can take away our burdens exists in several cultures. I visited one such tree in Korea where you could leave your anxieties, request some change in your life, or leave a message in the bark about a secret – very much a multi-purpose tree!

Exercise 7.9: Dancing for Freedom 1

Aims

- to get the body moving and physically displace anxiety
- to integrate mind and body to transform anxious states

Resources

- mat
- rhythmic music
- small scarves and shakers or maracas

Focus

Think about music that has a strong rhythm that encourages you to move.

Introduction

Recent research, whether in psychiatry or with older people with dementia, points towards dance being very important for the body as well as the brain. Rhythmic dancing in particular integrates movement as well as sound, and encourages self-esteem and confidence. Those teenagers who don't dance avoid it because they don't feel 'good enough'. I'm sure that we can all relate to that from our own teenage years – being nervous in case we got the steps wrong or were wearing the wrong outfit or just didn't appear cool!

To Do

Sit comfortably, and focus on calm breathing. Wait for the music to start.

- Listen to the music, and allow your hands and fingers to move to the rhythm.
- Now let your arms be involved, and just move in whichever direction you choose.
- Shake the maracas or wave the scarves to the music, and move your shoulders from side to side or up and down.
- Twist your waist from side to side, allowing your elbows to lead the way, still shaking the maracas or waving the scarves.
- Finally, swing your feet and legs backwards and forwards, with some final shakes, then be quite still and make sure your breathing is still calm.

To Think About

If we are anxious and terrified of moving, then we should start in our chairs or on our mat. That first step into space is a huge commitment, and needs lots of preparation. We may need to chair dance for a time until we feel OK about moving in space. This is especially the case if we haven't done any dancing when we were younger.

Exercise 7.10: Dancing for Freedom 2

Aims

- to encourage dance as a means of reducing anxiety
- to build confidence in the movement to rhythmic music

Resources

- mat
- rhythmic music
- small scarves and shakers or maracas

Focus

Concentrate on the rhythm of the music, and imagine moving to it.

Introduction

The step in this exercise should not be pushed. If we still feel like being glued to our chairs, that's fine. We can find other ways to sit and dance, such as straddling the chair and dancing our fingers along the back. The music needs to have a persistent rhythm that people can absorb and feel confident about moving to. They need to have some choice of the music – the only rule is that it must be danceable!

To Do

Sit calmly, breathe deeply, and listen to the music.

- Stand up, and walk across the space in time to the music – if you're in a group, then walk with a partner if you want.
- Try to move with your whole body – your arms as well as your hips.
- Use the maracas or scarves to emphasise the rhythm.
- If you know the tune, hum along to it as you move.
- What happens if you move twice as fast?

To Think About

Perhaps we need reassuring that we don't have to be dance experts just to enjoy moving to music. The TV is full of programmes and competitions where people have to vie with each other in technique, costumes, and special effects, and people are often ridiculed in the process. Perhaps we need a conscious effort to bring back dancing for fun!

CBT Exercises

1. Sit quietly, and imagine your anxiety as a large parcel tied up with string, and strong adhesive tape. It is too heavy to carry in your hands, so it is in a rucksack on your back. You feel very strong, and untie the straps so it falls away.
2. Create a picture in your head that all your worries are growing like plants, bigger and bigger. Soon, they are taller than you are. But you have magical powers, and one big blow destroys them forever.

Working Online

Imagination works well online. Working individually or in groups, both children and young are able to follow creative visualisations as well as the CBT techniques. Children, in particular, enjoy the idea of having magical powers!

Summary

Chapter 7 was about recognising the burden of anxiety and how it can take over our lives. We may become more and more dictated to by our worries, and they can sap our energy and control our waking – and sometimes sleeping – hours.

Questions and Reflections for Discussion

1. How must it feel to have the weight of a burden on your back?
2. Experiment with dancing to freedom.
3. What age do you feel most of the time?
4. What is the significance of holding on to your worries?
5. Did other members of your family have big worry burdens?

Chapter 8

Mandalas and Mantras

This chapter is mainly concerned with enabling children and teenagers to deal with their anxiety and move on – in particular, creating Mandalas is a means of recognising skills and strengths and releasing latent creativity. Mandalas provide a projective exercise that I have used with children of all ages and young people – teachers looked askance that I used the Mandala exercise with children as young as 5 years! The more that children can develop skills to manage their lives, the more they are able to self-regulate. This experience can be consolidated in older children and young people in order for life to become a slowly evolving canvas that they will gradually feel at home in, all part of their social development.

As Asquith (2020, p.54) says: 'Social Development might be defined by psychologists as the gradual gaining of skills, relationships, and attitudes, enabling us to make friends, to interact with others and become a member of society.'

Example

A group of Asian teachers were learning skills of Embodiment-Projection-Role and applied the techniques directly with the children in the special school nearby. The teaching session was on applying the Mandala Method, and the group enjoyed the session, but said it was too difficult for the children to understand. I said it was possible to introduce it to children from 5 years onwards. They disagreed, and in the following session more or less watched while I failed! One girl drew a smiling girl in the section where people draw their fears. Her teacher said in my ear, 'Told you so, she doesn't get it.' I asked the girl about the scary times, and she said that it was very frightening when her dad came home drunk and beat up her mother. So I said, 'And the smiling face?'

'Oh that's me, last night the police came and arrested him, so I'm very happy!'

– It is so easy to think that children don't understand!

Note

Exercises 8.1 and 8.2 should be completed one after the other, and are linked in content and structure.

Exercise 8.1: Mandala 1

Aims

- to provide a structure that contains people's experiences
- to encourage exploration of personal strengths

Resources

- shawl or cotton blanket
- mat
- crayons or coloured pens
- Worksheet 19: Mandala 1: Personal Strengths (see page 122)

Focus

Reflect on your positive qualities and how they can be strengthened.

DOI: 10.4324/9781032256641-12

Introduction

By focusing on personal strengths, we can build up more energy to challenge our anxieties and reduce their potency. Our personal development needs to be enhanced by repeating our positive qualities in various ways so we can overcome our worries and anxieties. These methods can include pictures, chants, and other repetition.

To Do

Sit comfortably, breathing calmly, with crayons or coloured pens and Worksheet 19 nearby.

- Read through the different sections of Worksheet 19.
- Either write or draw and colour pictures in each section.
- Reflect carefully on each section as you write or draw.
- Think about which was the most difficult to fill in, and which was the easiest.
- Allow yourself to feel positive about your descriptions of your strengths.

To Think About

'Mandala' is a Sanskrit word meaning 'whole or wholeness'. The diagram on Worksheet 19 gives the opportunity to express a balanced view of our whole self from several perspectives: our fears, skills, playfulness, and who inspires us. And very importantly, the centre space allows us to reflect on our identity in a positive way.

Exercise 8.2: Mandala 2

Note

This Mandala exercise should not be attempted unless Exercise 8.1 has been completed.

Aims

- to encourage people to express their anxieties in more detail
- to allow time and space to be more flexible about their anxieties

Resources

- shawl or cotton blanket
- mat
- crayons or coloured pens
- Worksheet 20: Mandala 2: Anxieties and Worries (see page 123)

Focus

Allow yourself to think about your worries a little bit at a time.

Introduction

This exercise is a first step in being more concrete about naming worries. It is intended to be used as a balancing exercise with Exercise 8.1 to enable us to hold 'the good and the bad' at the same time. It takes some practice!

To Do

Sit comfortably, and make sure your breathing is steady and calm – if it starts to change, stop the exercise and re-establish your breathing. Sit comfortably with crayons or coloured pens and Worksheet 20 nearby.

- Read through Worksheet 20 carefully.
- If any of the sections make you feel anxious, ignore them.
- Choose one or two to fill in with words or colours (check your breathing).

- Place the Mandala from this exercise side by side with the one from Exercise 8.1, and look at the differences and contrasts.
- What qualities in Mandala 1 could help the feelings or thoughts in Mandala 2?

To Think About

This exercise is known as a 'feeding exercise', meaning that the energy depleted by the worries can be replenished by the positive images in Mandala 1. As a metaphor, it comes back to the original premise of nurture which lies at the core of this book. In these Mandala exercises, we are learning about self-nurture as well as balance.

Exercise 8.3: Mandala 3

As earlier, this exercise should not be completed before Exercise 8.1.

Aims

- to encourage awareness of other people's perceptions
- to separate out self-perceptions from those held by others

Resources

- shawl or cotton blanket
- mat
- crayons or coloured pens
- Worksheet 21: Mandala 3: How Others See Me (see page 124) and a copy of your Mandala from Worksheet 19

Focus

Try to move from your own views about yourself to how you think others see you.

Introduction

We all have thoughts about how others see us. Some of them may be rooted in reality, and some in our own imagination. Families are particularly skilled in imposing stereotypes on family members, and once fixed, they are hard to remove.

To Do

Sit comfortably, making sure your breathing is calm and even, with crayons or coloured pens and Worksheet 21 and a copy of your Mandala from Worksheet 19 nearby.

- Read through Worksheet 21, and take some time to think about it.
- Decide which sections you would like to draw and colour or write in.
- The important thing is how you feel about these perceptions.
- Maybe people actually said them, or you imagined they said them.
- Place your new Mandala next to the one from Worksheet 19, and look for any connections.

To Think About

It is difficult if we feel certain that someone has an opinion about us, to consider that it might be in our heads! Where did the thought come from in the first place? Maybe we misunderstood something or maybe we did hear the phrase. Allow different thoughts to drift through our mind and in the end, decide how important is it anyway?

Exercise 8.4: Mandala 4

Note

As earlier, this exercise should not be completed before Exercise 8.1.

Aims

- to encourage some forward-thinking about life without anxiety
- to allow the possibility that the anxiety could diminish

Resources

- shawl or cotton blanket
- mat
- crayons or coloured pens
- Worksheet 22: Mandala 4: Future Thoughts (see page 125) and a copy of your Mandala from Worksheet 19

Focus

Imagine how life might be without anxiety – might there be a black hole?

Introduction

Anxiety keeps us trapped in the present. We dare not think about the future or plan new developments because our anxiety keeps us within a circle of fear and 'What ifs' – now we are daring to lift the curtain a little on what our future could look like!

To Do

Sit comfortably, making sure your breathing is calm and even, and have crayons or coloured pens and Worksheet 22 nearby.

- Allow yourself to think about the possibility of life without worries (if you get anxious about that thought, re-establish your calm breathing).
- Read through Worksheet 22, and reflect on each space in the Mandala – how do you feel?
- See how many of the spaces you can draw and colour or write in – it is important to fill in the central circle.
- Reassure yourself that these are just some ideas – you do not have to implement them!
- Place your new Mandala next to Mandala 1 and compare the similarities and differences.

To Think About

When we are in a state of anxiety, we often stop planning events or accepting invitations. We have created a status quo that we can manage, and we maintain its borders as strongly as possible. Once we start to consider the future, all sorts of things become possible, and it can be quite overwhelming. This is why Mandala 4 has some small steps in it, and not revolutionary changes.

Exercise 8.5: Mandala Reflections

Aims

- to integrate the insights from all the Mandala pictures
- to allow connections between different images and statements

Resources

- shawl or cotton blanket
- mat
- crayons or coloured pens and lead pencil
- copies of all four completed Mandalas from Worksheets 19–22

Focus

Free your mind to wander through the different pictures you have created.

Introduction

It is important to encourage some threads to develop as we see connections between things we say or draw or write. The use of the worksheets makes our thoughts more concrete so we can allow more flexibility.

To Do

Sit comfortably and calmly, and breathe in through your nose and out through your mouth.

- Spread your four Mandalas from Worksheets 19–22 in a line in front of you.
- Let your mind wander freely through them.
- Now specifically go from one sheet to the next.
- Note any connections between the worksheets, and make notes if you wish.
- Allow yourself to breathe in the learning, keeping calm during the process.

To Think About

It is easy to keep ourselves on a single-thread journey as if life is a straight line. However, we need to move on to experience the multiple threads and the twists and turns that make up the reality of our life. Sometimes it is all too much, and we get overwhelmed. By using relatively structured diagrams to explore a thread at a time, we can guard against there being too much all at once.

Exercise 8.6: Mandala 5

Aims

- to create something lovely for its own sake
- to acknowledge the joyousness that can come through creativity

Resources

- shawl or cotton blanket
- mat
- crayons or coloured pens
- Worksheet 23: Mandala 5: Creative Colouring (see page 126)

Focus

Try to concentrate on your own creativity and what it can do.

Introduction

After we have been through worries and anxieties and explored them in different media, it is important to take time out and do something for its own sake. Colouring in is safe and contained, but also allows scope for choices.

To Do

Sit calmly, making sure your breathing is calm and even, with crayons or coloured pens and Worksheet 23 nearby.

- Look at this new Mandala on Worksheet 23, and its shapes and curves.
- It may not be your favourite picture, but let it be good enough for now.
- Decide what colours you would like to use, then colour in the picture, noting how you feel as you complete each section.
- When you have finished, hold your new Mandala in front of you and take pleasure in your creation.

To Think About

Colouring books for teenagers and adults have become very popular. They sell very well at airports as well as craft shops. There is something very soothing about filling in the spaces, but choosing the colours ourselves. Mandalas have repetitive patterns and shapes, and it seems it is this repetition that is particularly soothing.

Exercise 8.7: Sound Repetition

Aims

- to show how the repetition of sound can soothe
- to develop ideas in sound and music

Resources

- shawl or cotton blanket
- mat
- Worksheet 24: Wizard of Oz 1: Protective Chant (see page 127)

Focus

Think about the rhythms you encounter in everyday life.

Introduction

Repetition brings security, whether we are rocking, marching, or chanting. Sometimes, the repetition can take over and become destructive. However, cultural rhythms are a part of rituals which are secure dramas that mark our life events – naming ceremonies, birthdays, weddings, etc.

To Do

Sit calmly.

- Notice how we breathe in a regular rhythm, a steady in and out. If we are anxious, it tends to get dysregulated.
- While you are breathing rhythmically, locate your heartbeat and notice its steady pulsing.
- Look at Worksheet 24, and slowly say the words to yourself and notice how they have their own rhythm.
- If that feels OK, say them louder, and if you are in a group, all say them together: 'Lions and Tigers and Bears, Oh My!'
- Although the chant mentions scary animals, the three friends, Dorothy, Scarecrow, and Tin Man, chant the words to get them through the scary forest.

To Think About

When we are scared or anxious, we can sing chant or whistle in order to disperse our fears. It works even better if we are with other people. In Story Sheet 4: The Buried Moon (see page 137), the brave villagers hold pebbles in their mouths to stop them from crying out in alarm!

Exercise 8.8: Repetitive Songs

Aims

- to raise awareness of rhythmic songs that soothe
- to encourage confidence in singing for comfort

Resources

- shawl or cotton blanket
- mat

- personal choice of rhythmic music
- crayons or coloured pens
- Worksheet 25: Wizard of Oz 2: The Characters Who Are Anxious (see page 128) and Story Sheet 9: The Wizard of Oz (see page 142)

Focus

Hum to yourself any tune or song that you enjoy.

Introduction

It is rare for us not to have a special tune that we hum while we work or walk. How frustrating it is when schools don't allow humming or singing to counter nervousness, as it encourages young people to focus.

To Do

Sit comfortably, settle your breathing pattern, and give a big sigh – this will help you to relax your chest and jaw. Have crayons or coloured pens and Worksheet 25 nearby.

- Read through Worksheet 25 slowly while playing your music choice.
- Read Story Sheet 9: The Wizard of Oz.
- Think about the descriptions of the four characters.
- They are all searching for something – and want the wizard to give it to them.
- Which of their needs can you identify with?
- Colour in the character you feel closest to.

To Think About

Do we feel we can concentrate better if we listen to music? I am not referring to the muzak that is played in shopping malls or background music in supermarkets. It seems that music of our own personal choice can help calm our inner rhythms and help us to focus. So perhaps we need to re-think our antipathy to headphones, since they may be helping us to pay attention.

Exercise 8.9: Finding the Courage

Aims

- make use of an archetypal character to encourage change
- to understand that change takes courage

Resources

- shawl or cotton blanket
- mat
- Story Sheet 9: The Wizard of Oz (see page 142)

Focus

Reflect on the theme that change can be scary, so courage is needed.

Introduction

The character of the Lion in *The Wizard of Oz* demonstrates so many of the needs that we have when we are anxious people. He pretends to be strong, makes all sorts of threats about his prowess, bullies weaker or smaller creatures, but is immediately seen through by Dorothy. We don't want to admit we are scared, so we'll put on a show of strength! However, when our strength is called on in a crisis, we can prove to ourselves that we do have courage.

To Do

Sit comfortably, and breathe in through your nose and out through your mouth several times. Have Story Sheet 9 nearby.

- Relax and meditate on the word 'courage' – what does it mean to you?
- Who is the most courageous person you can think of?
- Read through the summary of the story, and concentrate on the Lion.
- The Lion knew he had no courage – until, of course, he had to help rescue Dorothy.
- Think about any personal links you can make with the Lion.

To Think About

In our culture, the very word 'coward' sends shivers down our spines. People were shot for cowardice during the First and Second World Wars – 'cowardice in the face of the enemy'. Nowadays, we still have a very militaristic view of cowardice – although, with a greater understanding of post-traumatic stress disorder, when people 'freeze' in the face of danger, it is known that it is out of their control.

Exercise 8.10: Theatre for Change

Aims

- to create a miniature theatre to show our dilemmas
- to practise a flexible attitude towards our personal story

Resources

- shawl or cotton blanket
- mat
- shoebox or similar container
- craft materials such as wool, fabric scraps, covered wire, card, white glue, scissors, stapler, and magazines for cutting out pictures

Focus

Think about your own life story, and imagine it could be a play in a theatre.

Introduction

Sometimes, the idea of performing in a theatre feels quite overwhelming if we are shy or anxious. The idea of standing up in front of others may be terrifying: we might be rooted to the spot, our capacity to speak might dry up, and generally we might literally have 'stage fright'. However, if all of that can be miniaturised, it becomes under our control and much, much smaller than ourselves.

To Do

Sit comfortably, and take deep breaths as you prepare for a new activity. Make sure you have all the craft materials available and that there is time to create your theatre without being rushed.

- Use the lid of the shoe box as the 'stage', and the rest of the box as the 'building'.
- You can cover it with paper or paint, and cut out people to stick on to the back of the theatre to create the audience.
- As you make and stick, think about what story you would like to tell and how many characters you will need.
- Make the people with the wire, wool, and scraps, and make sure there are courageous people as well as anxious ones.
- Tell your story through your little theatre.

To Think About

When we make things smaller, they become more manageable. A calf in a field is not as scary as a bull! A miniature theatre enables the paradox of acknowledging something of our own story while getting a perspective that is not overwhelming.

CBT Exercises

1. Take a copy of your Mandala from Worksheet 19 and some crayons or coloured pens, and write or draw in each section your skills and experience.
2. Practise repeating the things you are good at that you have written or drawn on your Mandala.

Working Online

The Mandala exercises adapt very well to online work, especially if you can let children or young people have copies of the worksheets in advance. Otherwise, they can be emailed as attachments if the family has a printer. Always check out the privacy of the venue – are people coming in and out, interrupting, or commenting inappropriately.

Summary

In Chapter 8, we have developed variations of the Mandala exercise, which is an excellent technique for developing personal and social skills. The Mandala Method helps to build confidence and reduce anxiety. The chants and repetitive mantras are tried and tested ways of establishing safe rhythms and security.

Questions and Reflections for Discussion

1. Think of a favourite rhyme you enjoyed as a child.
2. Did you ever sing to yourself when young, to keep yourself calm?
3. Have adults in your past praised your skills and achievements?
4. Or have they done the reverse, and criticised you?
5. Think what makes you feel good about yourself

Chapter 9

Masks and Flowers

This chapter connects us with positive images to replace negative ones that cause anxiety. It explores the idea of using masks to protect vulnerable feelings. It also recommends stories about growth and blossoms as a way of combating negative and empty feelings that lower our self-esteem.

In my book *101 Ideas for Positive Thoughts & Feelings* (Jennings 2014), I emphasise the importance of Positive Psychology (see Seligman 2011) for enhancing feelings of wellbeing. It's important to think about and reinforce what children can do, rather than what they can't do:

> Children and teenagers need the time and space, and empathic leadership, in order to express their feelings without fear of being ridiculed or judged. Too often issues are bottled up and may manifest themselves in eating difficulties, nightmares, insomnia, withdrawal, violent behaviour and more.
>
> (Jennings 2014, p.xii)

Exercise 9.1: My Mask of Safety

Aims

- to create a sense of protection of vulnerability
- to encourage flexibility in long-term anxiety

Resources

- shawl or cotton blanket
- mat
- coloured pens or crayons
- plain white mask (if available) or Worksheet 26: My Protective Mask (see page 129)

Focus

Think about creating protection for yourself if you are feeling vulnerable.

Introduction

Often when we are anxious, we can also feel very vulnerable, so the anxiety becomes a way of protecting ourselves. Maybe it would be helpful to develop a mask to protect ourselves which will allow us more movement and flexibility. The mask could be an actual mask, or a symbol of what we want to create.

To Do

Sit comfortably and breathe calmly with coloured pens or crayons and a blank mask or Worksheet 26 nearby.

- Keep breathing evenly, and think about the shape and colour of a protective mask.
- Draw and colour in a face and its expression on a blank mask or Worksheet 26.

DOI: 10.4324/9781032256641-13

- Remember that this is a protective mask, not an exposing mask.
- Put the mask in front of your own face, and if possible, look in a mirror.
- Check whether you feel comfortable that this is a protective mask for you.

To Think About

When we decide to change and let go of some of our anxiety, it is important that we are not left feeling exposed. Letting go of tension and worry has to be a slow process, or we may be left feeling very empty and without protection. The idea of the mask is one of the safeguards.

Exercise 9.2: Mask of Fears

Note

This exercise should not be attempted before completion of Exercise 9.1.

Aims

- to encourage people to name their fears
- to develop confidence in literally 'facing their fears'

Resources

- shawl or cotton blanket
- mat
- coloured pens or crayons
- plain white mask (if available) or Worksheet 26: My Protective Mask (see page 129)

Focus

While breathing calmly, allow yourself to reflect on some of the fears that make you feel anxious.

Introduction

The exploration of our fears needs to be gradual. It can be very helpful to create a mask that we can look at and hold in front of us, but also to be able take it away. By identifying our fears, we can place them alongside our protective masks so that we don't get too vulnerable.

To Do

Sit comfortably and breathe calmly, and have coloured pens or crayons and a blank mask or Worksheet 26 nearby.

- Be sure to maintain your calm breathing.
- Reflect on some of the fears that make you feel anxious.
- Draw and colour in a face on a blank mask or Worksheet 26 that shows some of these fears.
- Look at the face or mask alongside your first protective mask from Exercise 9.1.
- How are they different, and how might you change your first mask?

To Think About

By taking gradual steps to look at our fears, we can slowly let go of our anxiety. In this approach, we are not looking to explain our anxieties, we are looking to replace them with more positive thoughts and feelings. The more we can encourage a sense of nurture, the easier this will become.

Exercise 9.3: Mask of Change

Note

This exercise should not be attempted before completion of Exercise 9.1.

Aims

- to create the possibility of replacing our fears with positive thoughts
- to allow new ideas to develop strength over our anxieties

Resources

- shawl or cotton blanket
- mat
- coloured pens or crayons
- plain white mask (if available) or Worksheet 27: My Mask of Change (see page 130)

Focus

Think about how you would like to change your anxieties and fears.

Introduction

By using changing masks, we are able to look at possibilities for the future and whether we can replace our anxieties with more positive thinking. The masks can be created a step at a time and our progression throughout all the masks can show how we are building up our personal strength and willingness to change.

To Do

Sit comfortably, breathing calmly, with coloured pens or crayons and a blank mask or Worksheet 27 nearby.

- While breathing steadily, allow yourself to think about changes.
- Although our mask of fears from Exercise 9.2 may give us some security, how does it feel to let it go?
- If you could change your mask of fears, what would it look like?
- Now create the shapes and colours of your mask of change.
- Place it alongside your masks from Exercises 9.1 and 9.2, and look at their similarities and differences.

To Think About

We may feel our anxiety is a type of negative energy, but because it is familiar to us, it is easier to hold on to it. We need to be aware of the possibility of replacing our fears with other ideas, and looking at potential change is the first step in that direction.

Exercise 9.4: My Discarded Mask

Note

This exercise should not be attempted before completion of Exercise 9.1.

Aims

- to reinforce the idea of letting go of our anxiety
- to create images of negativity we would like to get rid of

Resources

- shawl or cotton blanket
- mat

- coloured pens or crayons
- plain white mask (if available) or Worksheet 28: My Discarded Mask (see page 131)

Focus

Reflect on the possibility of discarding negative feelings and replacing them with others.

Introduction

When we are ready to replace some of our anxiety with more positive thoughts and feelings, we can then think of discarding the anxiety. Creating a mask of what we are discarding makes the experience very 'concrete', rather than just a thought. The discarded mask can be looked at again in the future to see how much progress we have made in our recovery.

To Do

Sit comfortably, breathing calmly, with coloured pens or crayons and a blank mask or Worksheet 28 nearby.

- Take some very deep breaths in through your nose and out through your mouth, then give a big sigh.
- Bring to mind what you feel ready to let go of now in terms of your anxieties.
- Create a mask of your anxieties and what you are going to drop.
- Put this mask or face alongside the masks from Exercises 9.1–9.3, and look at their similarities or differences.
- If you think you have discarded too much too quickly, you can modify this last mask so it feels manageable.

To Think About

In creating the mask of what we will discard, we need to make sure we can identify our fears, but it is important we don't do it all at once. The fact that a mask of a face can be changed is very important in reinforcing the idea that nothing is fixed forever.

Exercise 9.5: My Beautiful Mask

Note

This exercise should not be attempted before completion of Exercise 9.1.

Aims

- to encourage celebration of change
- to make sure we can create something for its own sake

Resources

- shawl or cotton blanket
- mat
- coloured pens or crayons
- plain white mask (if available) or Worksheet 29: My Beautiful Mask (see page 132)

Focus

Think of a mask that for you would look very beautiful.

Introduction

It is important that we feel that creativity can be for its own sake, and not just to illustrate change. By making a beautiful mask, we are affirming our creativity and the idea that the world can be more beautiful than we used to think it was.

To Do

Sit comfortably and breathe calmly with coloured pens or crayons and a blank mask or Worksheet 29 nearby.

- Bring to mind the most beautiful mask you can think of – maybe it is very simple, maybe it is exotic, but it is your choice.
- Create a mask or face using the colours of your choice, and take your time to complete it.
- Place the mask from this exercise alongside those from Exercises 9.1–9.4, and look at your journey through the masks.
- Place the masks from Exercises 9.1, 9.3, and 9.5 side by side, and reflect on their positivity.

To Think About

By creating our own images of faces or masks, we can look at our potential and also our pace of change. People need time to let go of their masks of fear and their discarded masks. In time, they may feel they can let go of their mask of protection. It is very important that people can hold on to their changes, but also retain the positive mask for its own sake.

Exercise 9.6: Wasting Time on Special Things

Aims

- to encourage people to feel less pressurised in their achievements
- to encourage choices in how we spend our time

Resources

- shawl or cotton blanket
- mat
- Story Sheet 10: The Little Prince (see page 143)

Focus

Think about what you feel you ought to do and what you feel you would like to do.

Introduction

In the story of the Little Prince, we have a very good example of being able to waste time on something that is important to us. The fox advises the Little Prince that the most important thing is what you waste your time on. The Little Prince remembers the one little rose on his planet he looked after although she was rude and arrogant. When the Little Prince arrives on Earth, he finds a whole garden full of roses instead of his individual special one.

To Do

Sit comfortably, and breathe calmly.

- Read through Story Sheet 10: The Little Prince.
- Think about his special rose and what it meant to him.
- What do you feel about the advice of the fox – is it a good thing to waste time?
- How would it feel to spend some of your time on nothing in particular?
- Does that idea make you feel pleased, or anxious?

To Think About

We often feel that everything we do in life should be purposeful, achieving grades and passing exams, or making decisions about our careers, or living up to the expectations of our parents. The story of the Little Prince gives us freedom to think about these expectations, and whether in fact it would do us some good to 'waste some time'. Does every minute of every day have to be filled with prescriptive activities?

Exercise 9.7: My Special Object

Note

This activity can be linked to Exercise 9.8.

Aims

- to create something dear to us that is new and different
- to allow ourselves to have greater freedom of choice

Resources

- shawl or cotton blanket
- mat
- coloured pens or crayons
- blank paper
- Story Sheet 10: The Little Prince (see page 143)

Focus

Allow your mind to think about something new that could be very special.

Introduction

When we start to let go of unnecessary fears and feelings, we can begin to replace them with new thoughts and ideas. Like in the story of the Little Prince, we all need something that we can waste our time on, whether it is a hobby or an object. Maybe for some people, it could be a sport. The important thing is that we don't become obligated to this new activity, that we have freedom of choice.

To Do

Sit comfortably, and breathe calmly, with coloured pens or crayons, Story Sheet 10, and a blank sheet of paper nearby.

- Read through Story Sheet 10.
- In the story, the Little Prince had his rose. Think about something that you would like – it could be something growing, or it could be an activity or a hobby.
- Draw and colour this new idea.
- How does it feel to actually name it?
- Think about whether this will stay as just a thought, or whether you might put it in to action.

To Think About

It is very easy to get trapped into the rut of our job or studies and even the ruts of our anxieties. They hold on to us and stop us moving on. By giving ourselves permission to have a new interest, it will help us to free up in other areas of our lives too.

Exercise 9.8: Telling My Story

Aims

- to encourage storytelling about special things in our lives
- to acknowledge that things can be special, and therefore communicated

Resources

- shawl or cotton blanket
- mat

- coloured pens or crayons
- blank paper

Focus

Think about something in your life, or your choice of object in Exercise 9.7 that you think is special.

Introduction

If we are able to tell a story about an event or an object, or something that has happened to us, we are able to place it in a contained structure. We can then give it a beginning, a middle, and an end. However, when we are anxious, it may become a series of disconnected happenings, rather than something that has a narrative.

To Do

Sit comfortably, breathing calmly, with coloured pens or crayons and a blank sheet of paper nearby.

- Keep your breathing very calm, and think about either an event in your life or a new activity that you named in Exercise 9.7.
- In order to create a story, we need to move on from just naming whatever it was to describing what exactly happened.
- Create a story about your choice of new activity or the old event that has a beginning, middle, and end, – the story doesn't have to be long or clever or different.
- Write or draw your story using the coloured pens or crayons.

To Think About

The capacity to create a story is very freeing. It means we are able to communicate an event or a happening that is important to us. It also means we can begin to develop the art of storytelling for its own sake. Just as the Little Prince spent a lot of time on his rose, we can allow ourselves a lot of time to see what stories might develop.

Exercise 9.9: My Book Cover

Aims

- to find creative ways to contain our new experiences
- to use our imagination in different ways

Resources

- shawl or cotton blanket
- mat
- coloured pens or crayons

Focus

Having created a story of your choice in Exercise 9.8, think about how it would look if it was actually a book.

Introduction

Often, we can feel disappointed if our creative activity isn't contained in some way – a picture needs a frame, a story needs a cover. It is more satisfying if we can complete the activity in this way. Although the story created in Exercise 9.8 may have been short, it can still have a cover page.

To Do

Sit comfortably, breathing calmly, with coloured pens or crayons and a blank sheet of paper nearby.

- Reflect on the story you created in Exercise 9.8.
- What was the most important theme for you in this story?
- If this story had illustrations, what would they look like?
- Choose one to be the cover page of your story.
- Draw and colour your cover page.

To Think About

Moving from having created the story to drawing an illustration for a cover page is another step in affirming our creativity – the more we can replace our anxiety by both nurturing activities and then creative activities, the more we can feel confident in letting go of anxiety.

Exercise 9.10: The Return of the Flowers

Aims

- to find a story of rejuvenation to replace anxiety
- to experience a story that gives hope and creativity

Resources

- shawl or cotton blanket
- mat
- coloured pens or crayons
- blank paper
- modelling clay or plasticine
- Story Sheet 11: The Return of the Flowers (see page 144) and Worksheet 13: Journey to a Safe Place (see page 116)

Focus

Think about a garden that is empty of everything, where nothing is growing, and allow yourself to think about it full of blossoms and bushes and honey bees.

Introduction

In the story 'The Return of the Flowers', people experience the world as bare and desolate as the flowers and trees have all died apart from three sacred trees. The wise people of the village make the journey to the creator to ask whether he could send back the flowers. After a long and difficult journey, their wish is granted. They are able to bring back an abundance of flowers, the trees and the bushes return, and the people are very joyous.

To Do

Sit comfortably, breathing calmly, with coloured pens or crayons, paper, clay or plasticine, and Story Sheet 11 and Worksheet 13 nearby.

- Read or listen to the story 'The Return of the Flowers'.
- Think about a land with no flowers.
- Think of the longing of the village people to yet again have flowers and trees and honey bees.
- Using the coloured pens or crayons, create your own garden full of flowers now that they've returned, using whatever flowers and trees you choose.
- Reflect on the difference between the bare garden and the garden that now flourishes.
- Look at Worksheet 13, and use any of its ideas you like to create a drawing or a model of your own journey.

To Think About

This final story is a metaphor enabling us to think about the journey from emptiness to fertility. Maybe our anxiety has kept our life very empty of colour and growth and sweetness and light. If we are been able to shed some of our worries, perhaps our life can feel more colourful and more creative and sweeter.

CBT Exercises

1. Look through newspapers and magazines, and cut out faces that show a variety of expressions. Glue them to form a collage. Be aware of any expressions that you think could be you, and include positive as well as unhappy expressions.
2. Draw a face that shows your anxiety. Draw another face without anxiety. Think about the difference, and what you might do to change from one to the other.

Working Online

The mask exercises work well online. However, it is preferable to work with personally drawn masks rather than pre-printed masks. There is less control over the latter, and people may stay in the masks for too long. Using the ideas on the worksheets, suggest that individuals draw and colour the masks, and then hold them up and talk about them. End with a positive mask. Always allow enough time after the mask work for any calming which may be needed.

Summary

Chapter 9 has been about empowering people to develop their strengths and build their self-esteem. The Mandala Method is a well-developed technique that has been tested across different cultures and with age groups from 5 to 80. It is a very good self-help technique where people can allow their strengths to grow. Throughout, I acknowledge the importance of Positive Psychology (Seligman 2018) in encouraging more confident and optimistic children and young people.

Questions and Reflections for Discussion

1. Recall if you have ever had a garden of your own and whether you grew things.
2. Think about walking in nature as a means of reducing stress.
3. Find ways to bring nature indoors and enjoy the colours and scents.
4. Why is sand and water so popular with children?
5. Using crayons, draw and colour a picture of a forest.

Summary of Part III

Part III was about taking steps to replace negative energy with more positive activities. We acknowledge that maintaining anxiety is a very tiring process and that our wellbeing is enhanced once we begin to feel more positive towards life and living. Physical exercise improves our mindset, whether we are dancing or joining sports, or doing yoga – there are so many ways of engaging with our bodies in an energetic and focused way. We also know that the body is where everything begins! Our feelings and emotions, our beliefs and attitudes, our self-esteem and confidence all start in our bodies. Anxiety is located in our brain, how we think about something, which is then translated into bodily tension. If we change our bodily activity, we can change how we think!

Part IV

Resources

Introduction

As well as using these resources in teachers' workshops at school or with therapists, it can be helpful to prepare handouts for children and young people to take home. This will depend on the socio-economic situation at home, and careful wording will prevent parents feeling that you are being intrusive. A meeting with parents can be useful, or if it is a whole-class project, parents are more likely to participate. They could also be presented as some research about sleep patterns.

For instance, the following examples are ways to help children or young people to create a nurturing environment:

- Pyjamas that are fleecy and slippers that are soft or woolly will communicate care and nurture.
- If a hot water bottle is added next, we can be sure of continued warmth.
- It is now possible to get fleecy sheets for our bed. Having a duvet rather than blankets on our bed makes it possible to create a feeling of a nest.
- If we have four pillows, it is even better.
- We can also think about soft, cuddly toys. It was fine to have them when we were small, but we often feel shy about having them when we are older.
- One young woman who suffered from severe anxiety used to make a nest on her bed of about 20 cuddly toys, some furry and some velvet. She would curl up in her nest of soft animals and fall fast asleep.

As well as our clothes and our bedding, we can also think about the food we eat. Sometimes, food that is too hot and too spicy causes a bad reaction rather than a sense of being nurtured. A drink of hot chocolate can be very soothing, and it may also help us to relax. If we don't like milk, we can use hot lemon and honey, which has a similar effect. Food like porridge and cereal that goes soft when milk or fruit juice is added can be very soothing, especially when eaten warm.

In order to create your adult personal nest, think back to anything that felt soothing when you were a younger child. Is it something you have now or can acquire, maybe warm custard or tinned rice pudding? Many milky drinks or those with added milk can be soothing. If we have dairy allergies, the same effect can be created with soya, nut, or rice milk.

It's important to remember that we must not create situations that invite failure. All these ideas are merely suggestions, which may not be appropriate economically, culturally, or age-wise. They can also be applied in a creative class or individually, instead of at home.

DOI: 10.4324/9781032256641-14

Chapter 10

Worksheets 1–29

DOI: 10.4324/9781032256641-15

Worksheet I

Contract

GROUP CONTRACT FOR CONFIDENCE-BUILDING GROUP

1. We agree to meet weekly on ……. at …….

2. We agree to keep the things we share confidential

3. We know we do not have to do exercise that feel uncomfortable

4. We agree to support each other in building confidence

5. We agree to be kind to each other

Signed ………………

Date ………………..

Worksheet 2

Introduction to Creative Approaches

This introduction can be used with children and young people who are new to creative activities and for whom the idea may stimulate greater anxiety.

Explain that this is a practical session for people to try out, and that many people find doing these sorts of activities reduces their anxiety and helps them to control their panic attacks.

Have available shawls, cotton blankets, and mats so that participants have a choice of where to sit and are also able to cover up if they wish. Blank paper and some crayons or coloured pens will be needed for some of the exercises.

The Warm-up

Either use this exercise, or choose one from Appendix 1 if it feels more appropriate.

- Walk slowly around the room, and focus on being here in this space. As you walk, be aware of your breathing.
- Stop in a space, or sit down if you prefer.
- Breathe in through your nose, and blow the air out through your mouth.
- Remember that this breathing exercise can be done whenever you feel a panic approaching or if you feel stressed.
- Repeat the breathing three times, slowly and gently.

The Activity

Using the paper and crayons or coloured pens, just scribble or draw as you wish, using your favourite colours. Scribble gently at first, then use a lot more energy. If you are working in groups, sit with a partner and take it in turns to scribble and create a joint picture.

Sharing and Story

Invite people to share any ideas or activities they participate in that do not make them feel anxious. Think about whether the joint scribble can become an illustration for a story. Play with ideas for a short story – think about a short title like 'Splurge' for your story!

Conclude with a general discussion about meeting again to develop the work.

Worksheet 3

Cosy Places

Where is most cosy for you?

Please tick an option below, or write or draw your own answer.

( ) In my bedroom, because …

( ) In the living room, because …

( ) At the kitchen table with a hot drink, because …

( ) Somewhere else – draw or describe it.

Wherever it is, give yourself a few moments to imagine this place as you sit quietly. Close your eyes if you feel comfortable doing so, and try to recall the special nest and its atmosphere. Try to remember the special qualities it has that make it different from other places: its colours, textures, temperature, light and shade, and anything else that is significant.

Worksheet 4

The Nest

Draw or write about your nest – it can be an actual place or your ideal nest. What is in it, and what are its qualities?

Colour the nest in your own choice of colours.

Worksheet 5

Breath Waves

Imagine your breath coming out in wavy rather than straight lines.

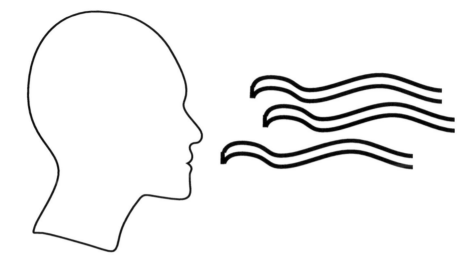

Worksheet 6

Lamps and Lights

Colour the lamp you like best.

Worksheet 7

Festivals of Light – Diwali

Diwali is celebrated by Hindu people, Jains, Sikhs, and some Buddhists.
Many cities have their own light festivals, with or without religious meaning.
The Lantern Festival is a Chinese festival of lights.

Worksheet 8

The Lighthouse

Colour the picture.

Worksheet 9

My Hand

Colour your hand as you see it.

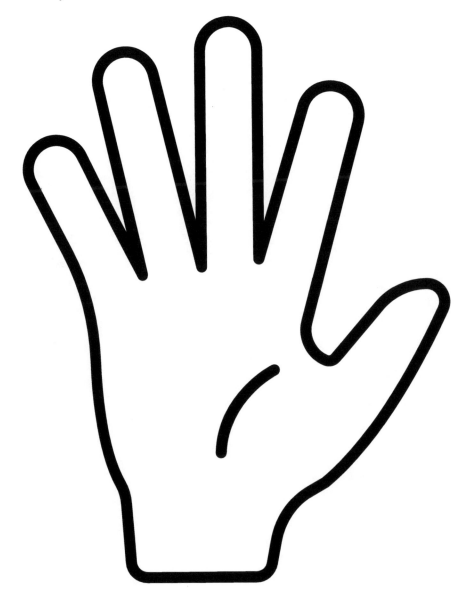

Worksheet 10

Silly and Funny Faces

Colour any faces that make you smile!

Worksheet 11

Different Facial Expressions

Colour any of the faces that especially catch your attention.

Worksheet 12

Different Facial Expressions (Cartoon Faces)

Colour these facial expressions, and imitate them in an exaggerated way.

Worksheet 13

Journey to a Safe Place

Create your own journey through drawing or painting, or make a model with clay or plasticine. Maybe you could include some of the following:

Worksheet 14

Bricks of Ice

Colour the pictures, and acknowledge how your body is feeling during the exercise.

Worksheet 15

Sisyphus and the Rock

Colour the pictures, and acknowledge how you are feeling about letting go of the heavy burden.

Worksheet 16

The Anxiety Balloon

Write or draw your anxieties inside the balloon, and colour it in.

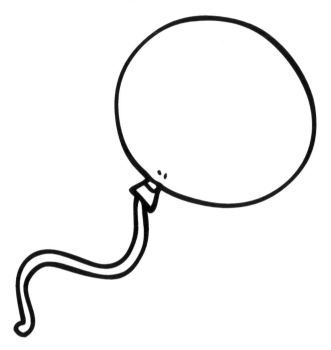

Worksheet 17

Dancing Demons

Colour in the demon of your anxieties, and see it getting smaller and smaller so that it will soon disappear.

Worksheet 18

The Tree of Worries

Colour in the tree, create your parcels of worries, and tie them with yellow ribbons to the tree branches.

Worksheet 19

Mandala 1: Personal Strengths

In the Mandala shape, write and/or draw and colour your answers in the numbered sections:

1. Who or what inspires me?
2. What am I good at? What are my skills?
3. What are my fears?
4. How am I playful or creative?
5. What do I believe in?

Apart from space no. 3, all the spaces should be positive statements about yourself.

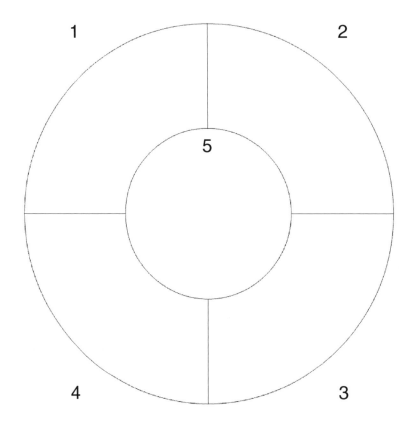

Worksheet 20

Mandala 2: Anxieties and Worries

Use the same Mandala shape, and in the numbered sections write, colour, or both:

1. people who frighten you
2. skills you struggle with
3. nightmares and scary events
4. creativity/play tasks that you don't complete
5. positive things you believe in

Colour and write in all the spaces in this Mandala, but stop if you feel uncomfortable. Start with the centre circle first: positive things you believe in.

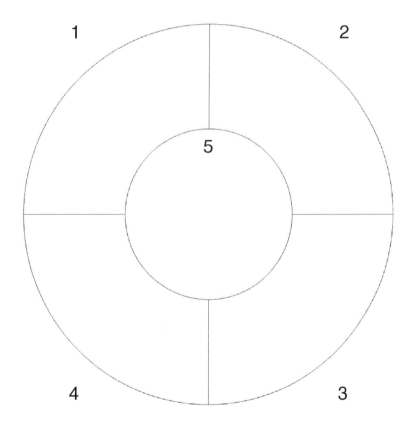

Worksheet 21

Mandala 3: How Others See Me

Use the same Mandala shape, and write or colour in the following in the numbered sections:

1. your parents
2. your teachers
3. negative people
4. your friends
5. positive people who believe in you

Colour and write in all the spaces in this Mandala, but stop if you feel uncomfortable. Start with the centre circle first: positive people who believe in you.

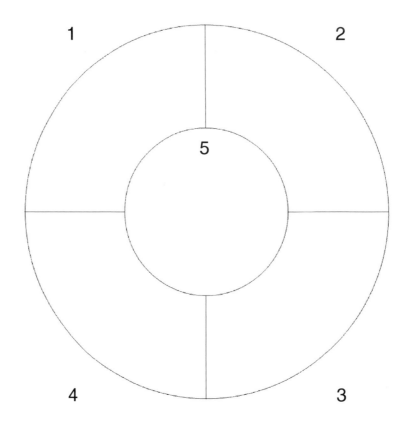

Worksheet 22

Mandala 4: Future Thoughts

Use the same Mandala shape, and write or colour in the following in the numbered sections:

1. special friend who will be a guide
2. new skills that could change my studies or work
3. a book or film that could help me deal with scary shadows
4. something artistic/creative that could help me be playful
5. friends who are supportive

Colour and write in all the spaces in this Mandala, but stop if you feel uncomfortable. Start with the centre circle first: friends who are supportive.

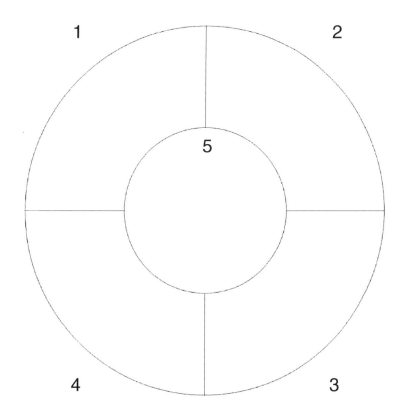

Worksheet 23

Mandala 5: Creative Colouring

Time to create something special! Use the whole Mandala to create a beautiful picture.

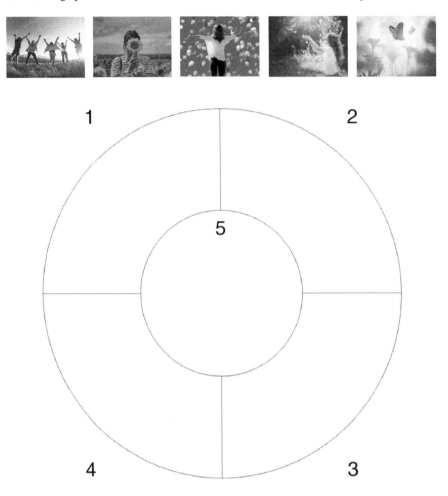

Worksheet 24

Wizard of Oz 1: Protective Chant

'Lions and Tigers and Bears, Oh My'

   Colour the characters and surroundings while repeating the words of the chant – remember that they are really scared!

Worksheet 25

Wizard of Oz 2: The Characters Who Are Anxious

Recognise that all these characters want something from life. Write them all down, and reflect on whether you have wished for the same things.

Worksheet 26

My Protective Mask

Colour in the mask, but remember it is your protective mask, so choose your colours and shapes carefully.

Worksheet 27

My Mask of Change

Create your mask of change, and include new colours and shapes to illustrate the changes in your life right now

Worksheet 28

My Discarded Mask

Colour your mask, and add symbols that represent the things you are discarding. Be aware of your feelings that at last you can let go of things that are holding you back.

Worksheet 29

My Beautiful Mask

Colour your mask to make it as beautiful as you can. This is now you, and you are special!

Chapter 11

Story Sheets 1–11

These stories are linked to the exercises in particular parts and chapters. They can also be used in their own right as bedtime stories for children to relax and listen to, or as a basis for a drama class, where the story can be read and then explored. They can also be enacted non-verbally, or drawn, painted, or modelled.

DOI: 10.4324/9781032256641-16

Story Sheet 1

The Sewing of the Stars

In a small village in China, the children and young people were playing in the fields. Everyone was happy because their village had been chosen to hold the Big Festival, and many visitors would come. Suddenly, the children looked up and saw great holes in the sky! What would happen now if the sky had holes in it?

They all went to see Lee Lieu, the wise woman who lived at the edge of the village, and they told her about the holes. She smiled and reassured them, and said to go back home and to look out of their windows once it became dark.

The children really hoped things would be all right, and they did as she said. That night, they looked out of their windows up at the sky.

What a wondrous sight! Lee Lieu had sewn brilliant stars into all the holes in the sky, and now it was shining like a carpet of stars.

The Festival would be splendid after all, and all the children went to sleep very content.

Source: Adapted from a story told to Sue Jennings in Malaysia by a Chinese storyteller.

Story Sheet 2

The Lighthouse Keeper, Part 1

When there were lighthouse keepers to look after the lighthouses, before they were made electronic, there were stories that survive today about life in the lighthouse. Keepers would be taken to the lighthouse with a boatload of supplies and stay there for three months. They would light the lamps at night and put them out in the morning, and make sure that the reflectors were always cleaned.

Jem was used to his three-month stint, and would spend time fishing if the sea was calm, which gave him fresh food, and he would read a book or write his diary. On this particular day, when he went down the steps to fish, he noticed a large bundle near the rocks. He realised it was a seal, maybe exhausted from the storm last night. He picked it up tenderly, wrapped in his jacket, and carried it into the lighthouse. He realised it was a she-seal, alive, but without any sound or movement. He laid her on a mat and wrapped some cloth around her, and put a mug of water to her lips, which she drank. She opened her eyes and struggled to sit up. Jem stroked her and said soothing words to her so that she would not be frightened.

Jem found some dried fish amongst his food stores and fed it to her – she was obviously very hungry. She was beginning to look better, and now tried to roll off the mat and lollop around the room. She was obviously feeling better too, and Jem wondered whether she was well enough to return to the sea. He left the door open, but she showed no sign of leaving. From his luggage, he took his pair of slippers, and discovered a third slipper! So he started to play a game with the seal as she flip-flopped around the room: he threw the slipper, and she fetched it. Then he began to throw all the slippers, and she fetched them and placed them in a neat row. Each time he threw them, she retrieved them and placed them neatly.

It was time for food, and Jem made them both some supper and placed water for her to drink. He then climbed the spiral staircase to light the lamps, which would be the safety signal for the ships not to come too close to the treacherous rocks.

It was getting dark – time for bed, and the seal lay down on her mat and was soon sleeping, too.

The next morning, Jem rose with the dawn and went to put out the shipping lights. He came back down again to make breakfast, and to his surprise, the seal was nowhere to be seen. He searched all the nooks and crannies, and even outside on the rocks, but there was no sign of Flippy. He sat on the steps sadly and looked out to sea – he realised she must have returned to where she came from. Of course she must go back, he knew that. But his loneliness returned as he realised how much she had brightened up his day.

Note: These stories can be read or drawn, and are particularly useful for group discussion and creative writing.

Source: Adapted from 'The Lighthouse Keeper', in Duncan Williamson (1992/2005) *Tales of the Seal People: Scottish Folk Tales*, Northampton, MA: Interlink Books.

Story Sheet 3

The Lighthouse Keeper, Part 2

Each morning, Jem opened the door after he had extinguished the lights, and stared out to sea. He wondered to himself whether Flippy might return to see him. Today, it was very stormy and the wind was whipping up the waves to a great height – it would not be safe for seals anyway. It was only a few more weeks before he returned to the village and his family.

He had his breakfast and tidied up, and then decided to check the small windows – he might need to shut them, with this strong wind. He climbed up three floors, and as he tried to shut the window, a huge gust of wind blew him backwards and he pitched forward down the stairs, unable to stop himself.

He lay at the bottom with a gash on his head. He was sure he had a broken arm and plenty of bruises. He couldn't get up, and then he passed out from the pain. He came round, and could feel someone wiping his forehead. He thought he was dreaming as he saw a very lovely woman standing next to him. She told him that he had been badly injured and must rest. She helped him to his bed and pulled off his boots. Then she made him drink some bitter-tasting tea, but he knew it was right. She told him that she would set his broken arm and shoulder, and as he tried to speak, she put a finger on his lips and said that he must be quiet.

For several days he rested, then he suddenly worried about the lamps – what must have happened to them? She told him that she had seen to everything, turning on the lights at dusk and then turning them off again at dawn. Nothing had been missed!

Jem slowly regained his strength, and gradually was able to walk around his room, with a little help. His shoulder was comfortable, and the gash on his head was healing. Today, he would try lighting the lamps himself, and he carefully climbed the steps. She gave him a lovely supper and more of the bitter-tasting medicine. And he went fast asleep.

The next morning, he switched off the lights, and was obviously getting stronger and stronger. He looked around to find his new companion, but she was nowhere to be seen. How could she have left? There was no boat nearby or sign of another person. He went inside, pondering what had happened. He saw – by his bed – three slippers in a neat and tidy row! Three slippers all together!

And now he understood!

Note: These stories can be read or drawn, and are particularly useful for group discussion and creative writing.

Source: Adapted from Duncan Williamson (1992/2005) 'The Lighthouse Keeper', in *Tales of the Seal People: Scottish Folk Tales*, Northampton, MA: Interlink Books.

Story Sheet 4

The Buried Moon

The people of the village were used to the phases of the Moon – when she would be thin and new, then full and rounded, then slowly fading into the old Moon, and then a few days of darkness. During the dark stage, they would be particularly careful as they had to cross a perilous bog on their way in and out of the village. In the bog lived some vile creatures that would try and snatch their clothing or pull them into the stinking water.

The Moon always looked down kindly on the village, she cared for the people, and recently she had noticed that they were not looking as happy as usual. She decided to go down and have a closer look. She was walking across the bog, and her long cape became tangled in the sharp thorns on the bushes. The bog creatures rubbed their hands with glee and pulled at the thorns, and the Moon overbalanced into the filthy water. As she fell, a young man was returning to the village and noticed that it was unusually bright for a few seconds, and then dark again – pitch dark.

The villagers were worried that the dark time seemed to be much longer than usual. Might there be something wrong? They went to see the wise woman, and told her that the Moon seemed to be away from them. She said 'Indeed,' and that the Moon was in some sort of trouble and they must try to help. She instructed them that they must put pebbles in their mouths and take a piece of the rowan tree as protection. The young man suddenly remembered that he had seen the bright light before the total darkness – it must have been the Moon in the bog.

A group of people put stones in their mouths and went with their rowan twigs and firebrands to the bog, where the creatures were screeching and laughing that they had imprisoned the Moon. The people moved forward and together pushed away the stone that was holding the Moon down, and at that point they were blinded by a piercing light. And there was the Moon back in the sky again, shining down on them. They returned to the village, and some of them sure they had glimpsed a woman in a dark cloak, just briefly.

The bog people were furious that they had been robbed of their prey, and the village people became just that little bit more caring towards one another.

Source: Adapted from Alida Gersie (1992), *Storymaking in Bereavement: Dragons Fight in the Meadow*, London: Jessica Kingsley.

Story Sheet 5

Fetching the Fire from the Underworld

Everyone was cold and miserable, as they had no fire. They had to eat their food raw and huddle together to keep warm. There was nothing they could do in the evenings unless the Moon happened to be shining very brightly.

One day, one of them suggested that they go and ask advice from St Anthony, who lived a little way out of the village with his pet pig. He was working in his vegetable garden as they approached. 'Saint Anthony, Sir, we need to ask your advice. Everyone in the village is very miserable because they are so cold. Can you help us get some fire?'

St Anthony thought for a moment, and said, 'Go back to the village and gather together a large pile of wood. If I am successful, I will come and see you before sundown.'

The little group went back home, excited as they thought St Anthony might just solve their difficulty.

Meanwhile, St Anthony put on his cloak, took his long staff, and started on a journey to the underworld, accompanied by his pig. It was a difficult journey going down, down, into a very deep valley, and then down again. At last, he reached the door to Hades and knocked on the door with his staff. A small devil opened the door a crack, and then shut it, saying 'We don't want visitors,' then seeing the pig, it opened again and welcomed them in, shouting, 'Roast pig, roast pig!' to all the other little devils. Soon there was chaos as the devils were chasing the pig, the pig was knocking everything over, and Anthony just leaned on his staff, slowly turning it round in the fire. There was such mayhem that nobody noticed!

The little devils became more and more hysterical, and Anthony said to his pig, 'I think we had better go, I don't want them to catch you!' They both made a quick exit and started the long climb home. They reached the village, and everyone was waiting. They had built the large pile of wood, and Anthony thrust his staff into the centre and it immediately burst into flames. Everyone was very excited and began to dance.

'Now,' said St Anthony, 'light some branches and take them to the other villages so they too can share your fire.' They did so gladly, and Anthony and his pig went quietly back to their house and garden. There had been quite enough excitement for one day!

Note: The feast of St Antonio Abate is celebrated on 16 January each year in many Sardinian villages, with bonfires and masks.

Source: Adapted from an old Sardinian legend, 'The Rite of St Anthony's Fire', which was picked up by Sue Jennings on her storytelling travels.

Story Sheet 6

The Myth of Sisyphus

Although Sisyphus was considered an extremely clever mortal, he was also very foolish. He challenged the gods and their rules in many ways. Zeus was very angry because Sisyphus broke the rules of hospitality that strangers should be welcomed to a new city. Sisyphus lured people in and then had them killed.

There are many tales of his anti-social behaviour by the authors Homer and Camus and many others. What concerns us here is his eventual punishment in the underworld. He was condemned to undertake a fruitless task of pushing a heavy boulder up a hill and then watching as it rolled down again, and then to push it up again.

Sometimes when we are anxious, we give ourselves a very heavy burden to carry. Our shoulders are bowed, our arms ache, and our whole body feels tense.

Unlike Sisyphus, we can free ourselves from the burden of worry. We can let the boulder roll down the hill again and walk away from it!

We might even skip away!

Source: Adapted and re-framed by Sue Jennings from the Myth of Sisyphus.

Story Sheet 7

The Golden Bird of Burdens

Near the forest is a very old tree – it is so old that the grandmothers and grandfathers, great-grandmothers and great-grandfathers, and even further back to the great-great-great-greats have spoken of the old tree. It's as if it has always been there, and people refer to it as the Tree of Troubles. That is because people from far and near, old and young, come to the tree to share their worries and anxieties.

Usually, they write a message on a piece of paper, fold it in four, and then wrap it in a piece of yellow ribbon and tie it to the tree. Sometimes, people tuck it in the bark, and others write on a smooth river stone and tie that to the tree with the same sort of ribbon. If there have been many people passing by, the tree looks like a golden tree with so many ribbons decorating it.

Before sundown, a large bird flies out of the forest and comes to the tree. It is the Golden Bird of Burdens. It gently gathers up as many yellow-ribboned bundles as it can carry in its beak and claws. The messages on paper it drops over the dense forest, and the ones on stone it drops into the big river – the paper and stone are returning to their roots.

The bird saves all the yellow ribbons and flies further on, to the village near the mountains. The villagers are delighted as a cloud of yellow ribbons wafts slowly down. They all rush to catch them, young and old, and wave a thank you to the bird.

Now they can continue making their costumes and headdresses, decorated with the yellow ribbons that move when they are dancing. They are getting ready for the Summer Dance Celebration, which is a holiday for everyone.

Note: This story can be read out or enacted through movement, or you may wish to create a picture of the Tree of Troubles which can be coloured, showing all the yellow ribbons.

Source: Original story by Sue Jennings.

Story Sheet 8

Journey to a Safe Place

You are sitting comfortably and checking your breathing – in through your nose and blow it gently out through your mouth. You are making sure you are not in a draught or near distracting noises. It's time for your journey. The importance of this journey is that it feels safe and does not take you past any dangers or scary beings.

You decide – is it to be the fields, the forest, or the seashore? Maybe it is a city park? It's your decision! You can see yourself get up from where you are and choose a path to walk. The sun is just warm enough, and you are surrounded by wildlife, trees, and flowers. Even the city park has its share of birds and squirrels.

You know that it could be easy to drift off, as you are feeling very comfortable. You start to be aware of a hidden place – it could be behind some trees or a rock cave near the sea, or a pile of hay bales in the corner of the field, or a corner of a building that has been abandoned. You wander over, and then realise that you feel very, very tired. Maybe you could have just a short nap inside this hidden place. You crawl inside and make sure that you can't be seen. And immediately you fall asleep!

It is just a short nap, but you wake up feeling very refreshed. You have a stretch and a yawn, and now it is time to return home. You crawl out of the secret place, take one last look around so that you will remember it, and walk back the way you came.

You are back where you started, feeling calm and comfortable. You remember this place so that you can journey there another time. You slowly open your eyes, and have a stretch and a yawn in reality.

Time to finish.

Source: Original story by Sue Jennings.

Story Sheet 9

The Wizard of Oz

This is the central part of the story, and is the most relevant for our current work.

Dorothy and her little dog, Toto, are travelling along the Yellow Brick Road which she hopes will lead to the castle of the Wizard of Oz. It is understood that the Wizard can grant wishes to the people who go and see him.

She first meets the Scarecrow, who says that he needs a brain. He is also in danger of losing his stuffing, which becomes an issue later in the story. They decide to travel together to meet the Wizard. Further along the road, they meet the Tin Man, who is very rusty and can scarcely move. Dorothy manages to put oil on his joints, and as he starts to move and even dance, he explains that he wants a heart.

The three of them travel together through the magic forest, which is quite hostile and the trees throw fruit at them. Suddenly, they are surprised by the Lion, who pretends to be fierce, but actually he is terrified. He is looking for courage and is aware that lions should have courage and he doesn't have any – he explains that he is even frightened of his own shadow.

The four friends travel together and have scary adventures with the Wicked Witch, who has Dorothy kidnapped and then threatens to set Scarecrow on fire! Eventually, it all works out and they end up at Oz, looking for the Wizard. Although he is something of an imposter, they all manage to have their wishes granted and Dorothy is helped to find her way home!

Source: Adapted from the original story by L. Frank Baum (1901), *The Wonderful Wizard of Oz*, Chicago, IL: George M. Hill.

Story Sheet 10

The Little Prince

This age-old story by Antoine de Saint-Exupéry takes us on an enchanting journey with the Little Prince, who leaves his tiny planet and travels the universe, gaining wisdom along the way. Back home, he has a single rose bush who is vain and selfish and convinces him that she is one of a kind. So he looks after her with every tenderness, but eventually her behaviour drives him away. The Little Prince visits several planets, which are inhabited by all sorts of strange characters – a king, a conceited man, a merchant, and so on – who are all selfish and petty, and successfully convince the Little Prince that adults are narrowminded and strange.

When the Little Prince arrives on Earth, he comes across a whole field of rose bushes. He bemoans the fact that he spent so much time caring for his single rose now that he has discovered that she is not so unique after all.

However, the Little Prince meets a wise fox, who teaches him about trust and friendship. The fox's lessons help him realise that he loves his flower, and that she really is unique and special because of the relationship they share.

Source: Adapted from the original story by Antoine de Saint-Exupéry (1943), *The Little Prince*, New York: Harcourt, Brace & World.

Story Sheet 11

The Return of the Flowers

The land was bare without flowers or trees, as it had been left by the Creator-god when he departed the world. He kept three trees that were sacred to him where the bees still made honey and people told their children how the world once looked. The people suffered greatly with no colour or growth, and in time decided to journey with a request.

A small group of wise people walked a long and difficult path for days and nights until they came to the special mountain. They climbed until they nearly reached the top, and sent a message to the Creator-god that people were suffering from having no trees or flowers.

He sent a message to the wise people that they should be led to the land where the flowers bloomed continuously, and that they could carry as many flowers as they could hold, back to their people. The wise people picked enormous bunches of flowers and tree blossoms, and slowly managed the difficult path back to their home.

They gave everyone flowers, who in turn gave flowers to others, and soon you could see flowers right into the distance. And the trees grew from the blossoms, and the flowers multiplied many times. And the people were content – indeed, joyous – at the return of the flowers.

Source: Adapted with permission from Alida Gersie and Nancy King (1991), *Storymaking in Education and Therapy*, London: Jessica Kingsley.

Afterword

Reading this book has been, for me, a departure from my stereotypic views of 'youth' and what all too many young and growing people experience. Many of us hold unrealistic views about youth being all about boundless energy and the ability to bounce back fuelled by inexhaustible optimism. The other extreme is to see young people in a less fun-filled light and imbue them with negative perspectives such as their needing to be controlled, or as being disengaged, unreachable, and even threatening.

A 'healthy' young person ranges between these extremes, but doesn't remain in the superficiality or negativity of either. They are able to make choices, as part of their maturing process, about who they would like to be. In a healthy person, a sense of wellbeing is expressed through behaviour that they and others are happy with, according to their social contexts. It imparts a degree of confidence about engaging with the world and those near to them, and an ability to show resilience when this confidence takes the inevitable knocks which are so much part of normal life.

When I first became involved in psychiatric services, so many decades ago, mental health issues amongst young people, especially children, were almost unknown. I am not saying that they did not exist, but that they were barely recognised. In my three years of psychiatric nursing training, mental illness amongst children was not once referred to. The concept of wellbeing did not exist unless its absence was described amongst the very young as a 'failure to thrive'. At that time, however, anorexia nervosa was becoming more widely recognised and being identified in the main as a 'teenager's disease'. Since then, it is being increasingly diagnosed amongst younger children, and is, *par excellence*, a pathological manifestation of the rejection of self, or even the hatred and punishment of self, fuelled by the extreme anxiety of not 'measuring up' to some unachievable ideal.

Controlling one's food intake may appear to be the best solution in a world where nothing else is controllable and one's changing and fashion-defying physique seems out of control. Eating disorders are just one of the ways in which anxiety manifests, but perhaps the times in which we live contribute to the incidence of this debilitating illness and related syndromes such as body dysmorphic disorder.

Ever since fashion, as an industry with a potential for a huge profits, was able to target young people, the importance of appearance and body image was emphasised and exploited. As has been mentioned, this feature in young lives has become more entrenched by the growth of social media, and according to some, young people's dependence on this screen world has also become an addiction.

Everywhere, they are being bombarded by images of what they should look like, think like, and who they should emulate.

Adolescence is above all a time when young people experiment with carving out their own social and cultural niches – the peers, tastes, and fashions they hang out with – distinct from their childhood selves and from their immediate adults, and which all signify their development towards a sense of identity of which they are the authors. How stunting, then, for a young person who for reasons of social anxiety cannot participate in this essential transformative process. How limiting for children who cannot allow themselves to experience what others would not even consider risky activities – walking in open fields, swimming, going to a party.

The great strength of this book is that it is a manual for approaching the task of dealing with anxiety in a sensory and physical way. In our urban environments and screen-filled lives, we are becoming sensorily deprived, yet childhood and teenage anxiety is so often somatised or expressed in other physical ways. The exercises in this book teach us that our bodies can be our friends despite their disquieting changes in puberty or their lack of conforming to fashion-dictated 'norms'. This varied menu of suggested exercises and lifestyle-changing practices uses anxiety's strongest weapon against itself – addressing ritualistic practices that promote health and wellbeing, as opposed to the obsessively limiting regimes that anxiety sufferers impose upon themselves. The exercises are inherently beneficial in two ways. The first is that of enabling the development of a sense of agency and autonomy that comes with making and practising positive choices. These, in turn, are designed to open up the possibility of interacting in a stimulating and pleasurable way with the outside world through the senses. When this happens, the body is no longer the enemy, but a vehicle for agency and choice.

DOI: 10.4324/9781032256641-17

This journey allows an even bigger step – that of creativity. Whatever it is that is made, be it a mask, Mandala, or picture, the participant's agency is manifest. Those children or teenagers have created something outside themselves despite, or in defiance of, their troubled inner world. During that process and in the contemplation of what they have made, they have not been in the grip of anxiety, or have overcome it sufficiently to be able to follow the productive task. They have experienced being in an anxiety-free space, and know that the influence of this personal demon can also be controlled and that they need not be helpless in the face of it.

I am expecting that this handbook will also enable practitioners to counteract any feelings they may have of being overwhelmed by this devouring, insatiable enemy to wellbeing and health. It is a vital starting point for the gradual interventions that will allow interaction with the healthy self and a benign, nurturing world. It is also the beginning of the practitioner's creative journey, during which they may discover their own methods of using sensory awareness, and expressive exploration to liberate their participants from the burden of inappropriate and debilitating anxiety.

Sharon Jacksties, Post Grad Dip DTh, RPN, BA (Hons)

Warm-ups and Starters

The exercises in this appendix can be used as an introduction to active work or as a beginning for any of the activities in this book. Teenagers and children themselves can choose an activity that appeals to them, and can facilitate it in the group if they wish. This will help to develop their sense of autonomy as well as boost their self-esteem and confidence. Sometimes, they may design their own variation of an exercise, which should be encouraged. It fosters autonomy and decision-making, and is often a step from feeling anxious to feeling empowered.

Using the Warm-ups and Games

These exercises vary from a very simple walk to a more complex game. They are ideal as an introduction to 'action learning', and provide a basis for confidence-building. Their most important function is to 'warm-up' – to focus energy. When choosing warm-ups, it is important that they are linked to the activities in the group, and not chosen at random. A warm-up is just that – it warms up the body and the brain, ready for creative activity.

I usually start with physical warm-ups, because often there is surplus energy that needs to be focused and then transformed. My approach does not work with angry expressions for their own sake, such as smashing old china or breaking bricks – I use physical energy that expresses angry energy and then turns it into something else.

For example, a physical game of throwing and catching a softball focuses on scattered energy and allows it to become collaborative energy. A jog around the park encourages a 'feelgood' factor and prepares group members for focused group work. In all warm-ups, it is important to remember awareness of breathing, whether to create energy or to bring about relaxation.

Warm-up 1: Breathing and Voice 1

These exercises are to be repeated three or four times.

1. Breathe in through the nose to a count of 4 and out through the mouth to a count of 4; keep the shoulders relaxed and the tummy tucked in. Repeat with a pause for 4 counts between breathing in and out.
2. Take a deep breath in through the nose and breathe out on the word 'home'.
3. Say, 'ho, ho, ho', as loudly as possible; repeat more loudly and repeat more softly.

See also Warm-up 5: Breathing and Voice 2.

Warm-up 2: Strong Movement

1. Invite the group to scatter around the room, then call out 'Freeze!' – everyone stands absolutely still. Then call out 'Go!' and everyone moves again. Repeat several times until unison is achieved.
2. Encourage contrasts, such as running around in a circle and scattering all over the place.
3. Move around the room as if being blown.
4. Run around, and jump very high.
5. Stand absolutely still, and create silence.

Warm-up 3: Rhythm and Drum Work 1

1. Invite the group to sit in a circle and clap a simple rhythm until they are clapping in unison.
2. Divide the group in half, one clapping the first rhythm and the second the same rhythm, but twice as fast.
3. Play with the idea of different rhythms – invite the group to make suggestions.
4. Allow group members to use a drum and lead the rhythm – they lead, and the others copy.

5.   Use a drumming CD, and suggest that everyone copies a rhythm.

Warm-up 4: Rhythm and Drum Work 2

1.   Using a drumbeat, suggest everyone walks to the beat.
2.   Try marching to the drumbeat, first on the spot and then around the room.
3.   March with a partner, and synchronise your movements.
4.   March with three people to create a marching 'wheel' – the person in the centre marches on the spot, and the other two march around in a circle (quite a challenge!).
5.   Attempt to march backward, still marching in the wheel (a big challenge!).

Warm-up 5: Breathing and Voice 2

These exercises are to be repeated three or four times.

1.   Breathe in through the nose for a count of four, then out through the mouth for a count of four. Keep the shoulders relaxed and the tummy tucked in. Repeat with a pause for four counts between breathing in and out.
2.   Take a deep breath in through the nose, and breathe out on the word 'home'.
3.   Say 'ho, ho, ho' as loudly as possible, then repeat more loudly, and then repeat more softly.
4.   Repeat quickly 'red leather, yellow leather' five times, then ten times.
5.   Repeat quickly 'a clown with a crown' five times, then ten times.
6.   Talk nonsense language with a partner as quickly as possible, and then very slowly, as if feeling sleepy.

Warm-up 6: Physical Activity

1.   Throw a softball around the room to each other while running. Vary by throwing the ball while shouting the name of the person to catch it.
2.   Hold hands in a circle, and pull each way – keep the circle intact.
3.   Hold hands in a circle, and move over and under each other's arms until a tight knot is formed. Slowly undo the knot without letting go of the hands.
4.   Pass on a clap or pass on a rhythm to create a ripple effect as if it is continuous.
5.   Stand in a circle. Each person sits down, one at a time. If two go down at the same time, you have to start from the beginning again. Repeat the exercise, but stand up from a sitting position.

Warm-up 7: Synchronised Games

1.   Everyone stands in a large circle. Each person takes one step forward, but if two people move at the same time, the game starts again.
2.   Repeat the exercise by moving out of the circle, one step at a time.
3.   Everyone stands in a large circle and counts 'one, two, three, four'. On four, everyone looks at someone else. If two people are looking at each other, they change places. Keep repeating until there has been plenty of movement across the group.
4.   As a variation, going around the circle, each person says a number in sequence, starting from one. Then call out two numbers, and those people have to change places. A more difficult variation is to call out pairs of numbers, such as two and seven or four and eight, and those people have to change places. People should take care not to bump into each other when crossing the group.

Warm-up 8: Clapping and Rhythm

1.   Pass a single clap around the circle, one person following the next, in the same rhythm.
2.   Repeat in the opposite direction, varying the pace if the group is ready.
3.   Change to a double clap, and send it around in one direction.
4.   Vary the pace, and send it in the opposite direction.
5.   Change to a triple clap, and send it in one direction, at the same time sending a double clap in the opposite direction.

Warm-up 9: Chants and Rituals

1. Share the idea that certain jobs have their own chants, so that everyone works together – for example, pulling a rope or rowing a boat.
2. Invite everyone to sit in a circle and teach the chant 'Aayee oh, aayee oh, ay, ay, ay, ay, aayee oh'. Practise until synchronised.
3. Add the movement of rowing a boat to the rhythm. Practise until chant and movement are synchronised.
4. Remind the group that words have rhythms, and that chants are based on words and sounds. Invite members to think of phrases that others say, such as 'It's goodnight from him – and goodnight from me' or 'Nice to see you – to see you, nice!'
5. Introduce the theme of words and music having rhythms. Invite group members to think of music they like that has a strong rhythm and words, and practise it together.

Warm-up 10: Rhyming Words and Rhythmic Words

With a rhyming dictionary:

1. Invite the group to sit in a circle and clap while saying words that rhyme – for example, splat, mat, cat, rat … or hi, my, try, cry, fry …
2. Share words that have a strong rhythm, such as; dinner, dinner, dinner or hokey, cokey, cokey, cokey.
3. Invite everyone to make up two lines that rhyme, for example: 'I went to school and broke a rule' or 'I went to school and fell in a pool.' Encourage more and more nonsense – for example, 'I went to school, riding a mule.'
4. In pairs, write down (or just say) as many words as possible that rhyme with 'song' (one standard rhyming dictionary lists 21), then add slight pronunciation variations, such as 'tongue'.
5. Ask people to form pairs, and give them a first line, such as 'Today, I am going to cook a song.' Each pair adds three more lines that rhyme.

Warm-up 11: Relaxation

1. Practise deep breathing – breathe in through your nose, and blow out through your mouth, slowly and evenly.
2. Breathe in through your nose, hold for a count of five, then slowly blow out through your mouth.
3. Take a deep breath in, and hum a note until the breath is finished.
4. Take a deep breath in, hum and make a vowel sound 'ah'. Repeat with 'oo'. Repeat with 'ee'. Continue each sound until the breath is finished
5. Give a very big sigh – and another one!

Warm-up 12: Physical Warm-ups

1. Stretch upwards and outwards, and have a big yawn. Repeat.
2. In a sitting position or lying down, stretch your arms and legs, including your fingers and toes, and then release them. Repeat.
3. Lying down, imagine you have a marble on your ankle and you are going to will the marble to travel up to one side of your body and down the other. Initially, it won't travel far as this exercise needs a lot of concentration. However, with practice, you can feel your muscles twitch as the imaginary marble travels over them!
4. Standing or sitting, give your hands a good shake – first one, then the other, and then both together.
5. Alternate no. 4 with clenching your fingers and then releasing them.
6. Standing or sitting, press your foot forward, leaving your toes on the ground. Repeat.
7. Standing or sitting, press your foot up with only your heel on the ground. Repeat with alternate feet four times
8. Standing, holding on to a chair if needed, shake one foot vigorously, and then the other. Repeat twice with each foot.
9. Sitting or standing, raise both shoulders as high as possible, and then gently drop them so they are relaxed. Shrug again.
10. Sitting or standing, using both hands, massage the muscles in your face, jaw, cheeks, and forehead.

Warm-up 13: Mindfulness

1. Sitting or lying down, breathe evenly and focus on any sounds you can hear outside the room. Then concentrate on sounds inside the room. Then concentrate on sounds in your own body, such as your heartbeat or breathing.
2. Sitting or lying down, breathe evenly and try to focus on a single candle and its flame, which is slightly flickering.
3. Sitting or lying down, repeat no. 2, but see the shiny table that the candle is standing on, and see the reflection of the flame in the shiny surface – it is gently moving.
4. Sitting or lying down, breathe evenly and picture in your mind's eye a perfect rose. See its colour and shape, and whether it is in bud, open, or overblown.
5. Following no. 4, while sitting, draw a picture of your rose – maybe it is in a vase or on a rosebush or in your button-hole.

White Noise and the Circadian Rhythm

White Noise

White noise is a combination of all the sounds that humans can hear. There is much research on the benefits of white noise, and some people believe that it aids sleep, especially in small babies. The sleep colours are still new in research, and there is nothing conclusive at the moment. Much of this can be found online and in various articles on childcare. There are commercial CDs with white noise. However, it is perfectly possible to use everyday objects to create white noise, such as electric fans or hair dryers, and even the human voice! When a child is distressed, one can rock and say 'shh' repeatedly, and the child will usually calm.

Lullabies to soothe babies to sleep have been used for hundreds of years. They have proved effective when babies and children are anxious, ill, or fearful. The human voice has to be at the same level as the cries of the infant. Maybe we should be encouraging our capacity to soothe others, as a human contact, rather than rely on machines?

However, when using white noise to encourage babies to sleep, it should not be left on all night, and should be slowly turned down once sleep is induced. It should never be above 65 dB, or hearing damage could ensue.

The Temiars who live in the Malaysian rain forest are riverine people. They build their houses on the banks of the main rivers, or nearby, in Kelantan State. The gentle sound of the river flowing provides a soothing sound to sleep by. When I returned to live in the UK, it took some while to adjust to sleeping without the white noise from nature. In fact, I did not miss it until it was no longer there!

Circadian Rhythm

This is our 24-hour biological clock, which takes time to become established after birth as the infant has been in darkness for nine months. Energy and hormone levels change in the morning and at night-time in order for us to live life and complete tasks, and then to rest. The circadian rhythm is disrupted after long-haul flights or if we switch from day work to night work.

Bibliography

Asquith, S. (2020) *Self-regulation Skills in Young Children: Activities and Strategies for Practitioners and Parents*. London: Jessica Kingsley.

Baum, L.F. (1901) *The Wonderful Wizard of Oz*. Chicago, IL: George M. Hill.

Berger, R. and Lahad, M. (2013) *The Healing Forest in Post-crisis Work with Children: A Nature Therapy and Creative Arts Programme for Groups*. London: Jessica Kingsley.

Blades, J. (2021) *Making It: How Love, Kindness and Community Helped Me Repair My Life*. London: Bluebird.

Brooks, R. (2020) *The Trauma and Attachment Informed Classroom*. London: Jessica Kingsley.

Burns, C. (Ed.) (2018) *Trans Britain: Our Journey from the Shadows*. London: Unbound.

Dana, D. (2018) *The Polyvagal Theory in Therapy*. London: W.W. Norton.

Dana, D. (2021) *Anchored: How to Befriend Your Nervous System Using Polyvagal Theory*. Boulder, CO: Sounds True.

Dawson, J. (2021) *What's the T?* Leicester, UK: Wren & Rook.

Daykin, N. (2020) *Arts, Health and Well-being: A Critical Perspective on Research, Policy and Practice*. London: Routledge.

de Saint-Exupéry, A. (1943) *The Little Prince*. New York: Harcourt, Brace & World.

Ekman, P. (2003) *Unmasking the Face*. Los Altos, CA: ISHK/Malor Books.

Ekman, P. (2004/2007) *Emotions Revealed*. London: Orion/Phoenix.

Erikson, E. (1965/1995) *Childhood and Society*. London: Vintage Books.

Fitzpatrick, C. (2015) *A Short Introduction to Helping Young People Manage Anxiety*. London: Jessica Kingsley.

Gersie, A. (1992) *Storymaking in Bereavement: Dragons Fight in the Meadow*. London: Jessica Kingsley.

Gersie, A. and King, N. (1991) *Storymaking in Education and Therapy*. London: Jessica Kingsley.

Hardtmuth, T. (2021) *What Covid-19 Can Teach Us: Meeting the Virus with Fear or Informed Common Sense?* Stroud, UK: Interactions.

Hill, M. (2017) *The Positive Birth Book: A New Approach to Pregnancy, Birth and the Early Weeks*. London: Pinter & Martin.

Holmwood, C., Jennings, S., and Jacksties, S. (2022) *Routledge International Handbook of Therapeutic Stories and Storytelling*. London: Routledge.

Hunter, K. (2014) *Shakespeare's Heartbeat: Drama Games for Children with Autism*. London: Routledge.

Jennings, S. (1995) *Theatre, Ritual and Transformation: The Senoi Temiars*. London: Routledge.

Jennings, S. (1998) *Introduction to Developmental Play Therapy*. London: Jessica Kingsley.

Jennings, S. (2010) *Healthy Attachments and Neuro-Dramatic-Play*. London: Jessica Kingsley.

Jennings, S. (2013a) *Creative Ideas for Emotional Intelligence*. Buckingham, UK: Hinton House.

Jennings, S. (2013b) *101 Ideas for Empathy and Awareness*. Buckingham, UK: Hinton House.

Jennings, S. (2014) *101 Ideas for Positive Thoughts & Feelings*. Buckingham, UK: Hinton House.

Jennings, S. (2015) *101 Ideas for Increasing Focus & Motivation*. Buckingham, UK: Hinton House.

Jennings, S. (2017a) *Creative Play with Children at Risk*. Andover, UK: Routledge.

Jennings, S. (2017b) *Creative Storytelling with Children at Risk*. Andover, UK: Routledge.

Jennings, S. (2018) *Working with Attachment Difficulties with School-age Children: Practical and Creative Approaches*. Buckingham, UK: Hinton House.

Jennings, S. (2019) *Working with Attachment Difficulties with Teenagers: Practical and Creative Approaches*. Buckingham, UK: Hinton House.

Jennings, S. (2021) *Dancing into Life: A Practical NDP Course Book of Theory, Techniques, Ideas and Stories*. Wells, UK: Close Publications.

Kelly, B. (2020) *Coping with Coronavirus: How to Stay Calm and Protect Your Mental Health*. Newbridge, Ireland: Merrion Press.

Lewis, M. (2017) *Overcome Social Anxiety and Shyness: A Step-by-step Self Help Action Plan to Overcome Social Anxiety, Defeat Shyness and Create Confidence*. London: CreateSpace Independent Publishing Platform.

Lowenstein, L. (2002) *More Creative Interventions for Troubled Children and Youth*. Toronto, Canada: Champion Press.

Mardell, A. (2016) *The ABCs of LGBT+*. Miami, FL: Mango Media.

Mate, G. (2019) *When the Body Says No: The Cost of Hidden Stress*. London: Vermilion.

Moore, J. (2021) *Developing Secure Attachment through Play: Helping Vulnerable Children Build Their Social and Emotional Wellbeing*. Abingdon, UK: Routledge.

Owen, K. (Ed.) (2021) *Play in the Early Years*. London: SAGE.

Porges, S. (2011) *The Polyvagal Theory: Neurophysiological Foundations of Emotions, Attachment, Communication, and Self-regulation*. New York: W.W. Norton.

Porges, S. (2017) *The Pocket Guide to the Polyvagal Theory: The Transformative Power of Feeling Safe*. New York: W.W. Norton.

Savva, G. (28 April 2016) What Is Emotional Hypervigilance? *Counselling Directory*. Available at www.counselling-directory. org.uk/memberarticles/hair-trigger-stress-and-anxiety-hypervigilance.

Schmidt, R.E., Harvey, A.G., and der Linden, V. (7 December 2011) Cognitive and Affective Control in Insomnia, *Frontiers in Psychology* 2. Available at www.frontiersin.org/articles/10.3389/fpsyg.2011.00349/full.

Seligman, M. (2011) *Flourish: A New Understanding of Life's Greatest Goals*. London: Nicholas Brealey.

Seligman, M. (2018) *The Optimistic Child: A Revolutionary Approach to Raising Resilient Children*. New York: HarperCollins.

Smid, E. (2020) *Rainbow Village*. London: Jessica Kingsley.

Talbot, A. and Loy, N. (2021) *Puppy Faces Fears: A Story for Children with Anxiety about COVID-19*. London: independently published.

Thomas, D. (1954/2015) *Under Milk Wood: A Play for Voices*. London: Orion.

Vincent, B. (2018) *Transgender Health: A Practitioner's Guide to Binary and Non-binary Trans Patient Care*. London: Jessica Kingsley.

WHO (n.d.) Gender and Health. *World Health Organization*. Available at www.who.int/health-topics/gender#tab=tab_1.

Williamson, D. (1992/2005) The Lighthouse Keeper, in *Tales of the Seal People: Scottish Folk Tales*. Northampton, MA: Interlink Books.

Winnicott, D.W. (1971/1991/2005) *Playing and Reality*. London: Routledge.

Index

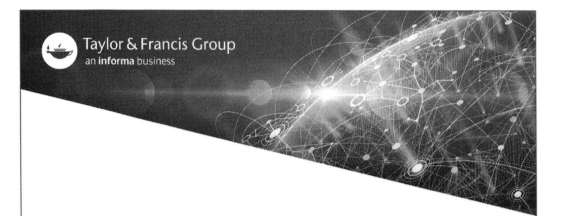

Printed in Great Britain
by Amazon

11120409R00099